THE
NEW LEADER'S
100 DAY
ACTION
PLAN

THE ONBOARDING PLAYBOOK USED
BY SUCCESSFUL LEADERS WORLDWIDE

THE
NEW LEADER'S
100 DAY
ACTION
PLAN

TAKE CHARGE, BUILD YOUR TEAM, AND DELIVER **BETTER RESULTS FASTER**

GEORGE B. BRADT · JAYME A. CHECK · JOHN A. LAWLER

FIFTH EDITION

FREE
DOWNLOADABLE
TOOLS

WILEY

Published by John Wiley & Sons, Inc., Hoboken, New Jersey.
Published simultaneously in Canada.

For general information on our other products and services or for technical support, please contact our Customer Care Department within the United States at (800) 762-2974, outside the United States at (317) 572-3993 or fax (317) 572-4002.

Wiley also publishes its books in a variety of electronic formats. Some content that appears in print may not be available in electronic formats. For more information about Wiley products, visit our web site at www.wiley.com.

Library of Congress Cataloging-in-Publication Data:

Names: Bradt, George B., author. | Check, Jayme A., author. | Lawler, John A., author.
Title: The new leader's 100-day action plan : take charge, build your team, and deliver better results faster / George B. Bradt, Jayme A. Check and John A. Lawler.
Description: Fifth edition. | Hoboken, New Jersey : John Wiley & Sons, Inc., [2022] | Includes bibliographical references and index.
Identifiers: LCCN 2022011368 (print) | LCCN 2022011369 (ebook) | ISBN 9781119884538 (cloth) | ISBN 9781119884552 (adobe pdf) | ISBN 9781119884545 (epub)
Subjects: LCSH: Leadership–Handbooks, manuals, etc.
Classification: LCC HD57.7 .B723 2022 (print) | LCC HD57.7 (ebook) | DDC 658.4/092–dc23/eng/20220309
LC record available at https://lccn.loc.gov/2022011368
LC ebook record available at https://lccn.loc.gov/2022011369

Cover Image: © Taphouse_Studios/Getty Images
Cover Design: Wiley

SKY10034034_051822

CONTENTS

We did not write this book as much as discover it. To a large degree, it is the product of all the transitions that have influenced all the people who have ever influenced us. Throughout our careers, we have learned by doing, by watching, and by interacting with a whole range of leaders—bosses, coaches, peers, subordinates, partners, and clients. We end every PrimeGenesis interaction with two questions: What was particularly valuable? How can we make it even more valuable? It is amazing what you can learn by asking.

What you have in your hands was born out of continuing to ask those questions and the realization that onboarding is a crucible of leadership. Done poorly, it results in a lot of pain for a lot of people. Done well, the benefits are amazing, positively transforming leaders, organizations, and teams.

We would need a separate book to credit all the people who have had the most positive influence on us over the years. But we must acknowledge the contributions of our past and current partners at PrimeGenesis. Their fingerprints are all over this book as we all work these ideas every day.

In particular, we thank Jorge Pedraza, who was one of the founding partners of PrimeGenesis and one of the original coauthors of this book through its first, second, and third editions.

We are indebted to the clients of PrimeGenesis on several levels. We are the first to admit that we have learned more from them than they have from us. We give our clients complete confidentiality, so we have masked individuals' and companies' names in the stories involving any of our clients. We are blessed to have the opportunity to work with an extremely diverse group of clients. They run the gamut from the multinational to the small, from public company to private, from for-profit to not-for-profit. The executives we work with come from many industries, from almost every discipline imaginable, and from many parts of the world. With every client, we have learned something new. Clients inspire, challenge, and teach us on a daily basis, and for that we are grateful. You can learn more about our list of clients on our website at www.PrimeGenesis.com.

We also thank the readers around the world whose enthusiastic embrace of the ideas in this book has kept us motivated to keep it current. We have the good fortune of truly engaged readers who download tools and interact with us on a daily basis from around the globe. We thank you for buying the book, passing it on, and reaching out to us to share your ideas, praise, constructive criticism, successes, and truly insightful questions.

Abounding gratitude to George's editors at *Forbes* starting with Fred Allen, and our editor at John Wiley & Sons, Richard Narramore. Each of them has nurtured our ideas and gently pushed us to make them better across the years.

And, finally, to our families and loved ones: We deeply appreciate your unending encouragement and support along the way.

Are you a veteran CEO taking the reins of your next organization? Starting a new role as a frontline supervisor? Something in between? Whether you are joining a new organization from the outside, getting promoted from within, leading a turnaround or transformation, or merging teams following an acquisition, *The New Leader's 100-Day Action Plan* will help you take charge, build your team, set direction, and deliver better results faster than anyone thought possible.

> *"We've found that 40 percent of executives hired at the senior level are pushed out, fail or quit within 18 months. It's expensive in terms of lost revenue. It's expensive in terms of the individual's hiring. It's damaging to morale."* Heidrick & Struggles, internal study of 20,000 searches[1]

If, after 100 days, a key stakeholder is asked, "How is that new leader doing?" and the answer is, "The jury is out," what that means is, "The jury is in, and we don't like the answer."

What do these failed leaders not see, know, do, and deliver? In most cases, they dig their own holes by missing one or more crucial steps in their first 100 days, including:

- Inadvertently sending their new colleagues the wrong messages and causing the culture to reject them

- Developing a new strategy but failing to get buy-in and build trust with their new team

- Failing to operationalize their strategy and deliver results

- Being too slow to make changes to the team

---

[1] CEO Kevin Kelly, as quoted in Brooke Masters, 2009, "Rise of a Headhunter," *Financial Times*, March 30.

- Expending energy on the wrong projects without accomplishing the one or two things that their most important stakeholders expected them to deliver

- Failing to adjust to changing circumstances once they're in the role

It's essential that you are aware of the important steps required to achieve a successful transition. No new leader wants to fail, but it happens at an alarming rate.

As an analogy, imagine you are driving from Ethiopia to Kenya. You get to the border in Moyale. You get out of your car to clear immigration. Once you clear, you get back in the car. You might think you can start the car, put your foot on the gas, and proceed to your final destination. But if you did that, you'd be sure to fail in a major way. Why?

Because the moment you've crossed the border, everything is different. In Ethiopia they drive on the right. In Kenya on the left. So, the first thing you must do is switch sides!

While there's no reason for you to have known that, you should realize that every organization drives on different sides of the road in different ways. If you don't figure out those differences and adjust for them, you're going to crash. This is why you must converge into a new organization and learn its unwritten rules and cultural realities before you pivot and lead it in a new direction.

Meanwhile, if you're operating in a business owned by a private equity firm, pressures can be even more intense. Gone are the days of delivering returns through debt and multiple arbitrages. To deliver competitive returns, you must create meaningful value through operational improvements or integration of accretive acquisitions in line with Figure 0.1.

FIGURE 0.1   Private Equity Buildup

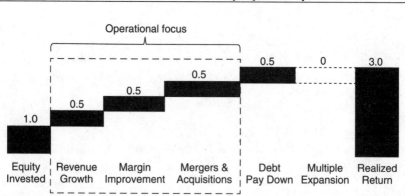

Perhaps not surprisingly, executive failure in private equity–owned businesses is even higher than average (almost 50 percent, according to a Bain study).[2] And the impact of that failure is stark and even more costly: Exits in these situations are typically delayed by 2 years, with reduced returns 46 percent of the time and longer hold periods 82 percent of the time.

Whether you are operating in a major corporation, a smaller start-up, or a midsize business, delivering value is not getting any easier, particularly where transformation and speed are musts. Failure rates are high—in addition to the 40 percent failure rate for leaders entering a new role, 83 percent of acquisitions fail to produce expected returns,[3] and only 26 percent of transformations are deemed very or completely successful.[4] But, this won't happen to you. Not if you let us help you.

Our fundamental, underlying concept is that onboarding is a crucible of leadership and that:

Leadership is about inspiring, enabling, and empowering others to do their absolute best together to realize a meaningful and rewarding shared purpose.

The Chinese philosopher Lao-tzu expressed this particularly well more than 2,500 years ago:

The great leader speaks little. He never speaks carelessly. He works without self-interest and leaves no trace. When all is finished, the people say, "We did it ourselves."[5]

With that in mind, *The New Leader's 100-Day Action Plan* is a practical playbook complete with the tools, action plans, timelines, and key milestones you need to reach along the way to accelerate your own and your team's success in your first 100 days and beyond.

Our insights are gleaned from our own leadership experiences and from the work of our firm, PrimeGenesis, whose sole mission is to

---

[2] Bain & Company, 2015, Global Private Equity Report, p. 56.
[3] KPMG study, reported by Margaret Heffernan, 2012, "Why Mergers Fail," *CBS Money Watch*, April 24.
[4] Study by Rajiv Chandran, Hortense de la Boutetier, and Carolyn Dewar, 2015, "Ascending to the C-Suite," *McKinsey Insights*, April.
[5] Paraphrasing the seventeenth verse of the Tao Te Ching by Lao-tzu.

help executives and teams deliver better results faster during critical transitions. Across all of our clients, the 100-Day Action Plan approach has reduced the failure rate for new leaders from the industry average of 40 percent to less than 10 percent. Our top 10 executive onboarding clients have deployed us more than 180 times.

Since 2003, leaders and teams in public multinationals, such as American Express and Johnson & Johnson; in midsize entities owned by private equity firms, such as MacAndrews & Forbes, Clayton, Dubilier & Rice, and Cerberus; and in not-for-profit organizations, such as the Red Cross, have implemented the 100-Day Action Plan. They have deployed it across a wide range of functions and complex transitions, including executive onboarding, turnarounds, reorganizations, transformations, and integrating leadership teams during acquisitions.

Over the years, we have noticed that many new leaders show up for a new role happy and smiling but without a plan. Neither they nor their organizations have thought things through in advance. On their first day, they are welcomed by such confidence-building remarks as: "Oh, you're here . . . we'd better find you an office."

Ouch!

Some enlightened organizations have a better process in place. They put people in charge of preparing for leaders' transitions. Imagine the difference when a new leader is escorted to an office that is fully set up for them, complete with computer, passwords, phones, files, information, and a 30-day schedule of orientation and assimilation meetings.

Better . . . but still not good enough.

Even if the company has set everything up for you, if you have waited until your first day on the job to start, you are already behind with the odds stacked against you. Paradoxically, the best way to accelerate a complex pivot like going into a new role is to pause long enough to think through a plan before you start, put it in place early, and then get a head start on implementing it.

As the leader, you must align all stakeholders around a shared purpose and set of objectives, set a compelling direction, build a cohesive leadership team, and create a culture that enables excellent execution.

As it turns out, these are some of the most difficult tasks faced by leaders entering complex situations, made even more challenging when compounded by the need for speed.

FIGURE 0.2 Converge and Evolve

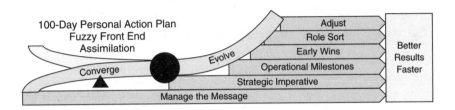

Having a process and set of tools can help you use your first 100 days to meet these challenges and propel you down the path to success (Figure 0.2).

The four main ideas are:

1. **Get a head start.** Day One is a critical pivot point for people moving into new roles or merging teams. In both situations, you can accelerate progress by hitting the ground running. Preparation in the days and weeks leading up to Day One breeds confidence, and a little early momentum goes a long way.

2. **Manage the message.** Everything communicates. People read things into everything you say and do and don't say and don't do. You're far better off choosing and guiding *what* others see and hear and *when* they see and hear it rather than leaving things up to chance or letting others make those choices for you. Start this process with your best current thinking on a headline message before Day One and adjust steadfastly as you go along.

3. **Set direction. Build the team.** The first 100 days are the best time to put in place the basic building blocks of a cohesive, high-performing team. You will fail if you try to create the organization's imperative yourself without the support and buy-in of your team. As team leader, your own success is inextricably linked to the success of the team as a whole.

4. **Sustain momentum. Deliver results.** Although the first 100 days are a sprint to jump-start communication, team building, and core practices, it's all for naught if you then sit back and watch things happen. You must evolve your leadership, practices, and culture to keep fueling the fires you sparked and deliver ongoing results.

These four ideas are built on the frameworks of highly effective teams and organizations and flow through the book. It's helpful to explain them up front. First, the headlines:

- High-performing teams and organizations are built of people, plans, and practices aligned around a shared purpose.

- Tactical capacity bridges the gap between strategy and execution, ensuring that a good strategy doesn't fail because of bad execution.

- Six building blocks underpin a team's tactical capacity: culture-shaping communication, burning imperative, milestone management, early wins, role sort, and then ongoing evolution.

People, Plans, Practices

Organization and team performance are based on aligning people, plans, and practices around a shared purpose. This involves getting strong people in the right roles with the right direction, resources, authority, and accountability; clarity around the strategies and action steps included in plans; and practices in place that enable people to work together in a systematic and effective way. The heart of this is a clearly understood, meaningful, and rewarding shared purpose.

Tactical Capacity

Tactical capacity is a team's ability to work under difficult, changing conditions and to translate strategies into tactical actions decisively, rapidly, and effectively. It is the essential bridge between strategy and execution (Figure 0.3).

In contrast to other work groups that move slowly, with lots of direction and most decision-making coming from the leader, high-performing teams with strong tactical capacity empower each member, communicate effectively with the team and leader to create critical solutions to the inevitable problems that arise on an ongoing basis and to implement them quickly.

The objective is high-quality responsiveness; it takes cohesive teamwork to make it happen. High-performing teams build on strategy and plans with strong people and practices to implement ever-evolving and acutely responsive actions that work.

FIGURE 0.3 Tactical Capacity

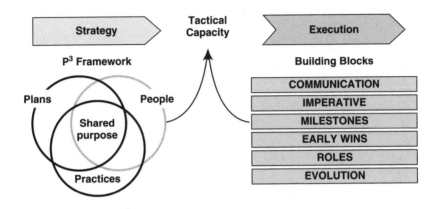

> *It is not the strongest of the species that survives, nor the most intelligent, but the one most responsive to change.*

> —Attributed to Charles Darwin

You probably have seen this yourself. You may have been on teams with members who operate in disconnected silos, incapable of acting without specific direction from above. They may know the strategy. They may have the resources they need, but any variation or change paralyzes them.

The Federal Emergency Management Agency (FEMA) actually had run the drill on a major hurricane in New Orleans months before Katrina hit. But the plan collapsed with the first puff of wind because no one could react flexibly and insightfully to a situation that was different from what they had expected.

In contrast, a great example of tactical capacity at work was the way the National Aeronautics and Space Administration (NASA) team members came together during the Apollo 13 crisis. Right from "Houston, we've had a problem," the team reacted flexibly and fluidly to a dramatic and unwelcome new reality—a crippling explosion en route, in space.

The team went beyond its standard operating procedures and what its equipment was "designed to do" to exploring what it "could do." Through tight, on-the-fly collaboration, the team did in minutes what normally took hours, in hours what normally took days, and in days what normally took months. The tactical capacity building blocks were critical to getting the crew home safely:

1. The culture had been strong. But everyone's *communication* reinforced the message that "failure is not an option" throughout the rescue mission.

2. The team's mission changed from "go to the moon to collect rocks" to the one *burning imperative* of "get these men home alive." This was galvanizing enough (as a burning imperative must always be) to transcend all petty issues and focus everyone's efforts.

3. The team's *milestones* were clear: Turn the ship around, preserve enough energy to allow a reentry, fix the carbon monoxide problem, survive the earth's atmosphere, and so on.

4. The carbon monoxide fix allowed the astronauts to stay alive and was the *early win* that made the team believe it could do the rest of the things that would get the crew back to Earth safely. It gave everyone confidence.

5. Everyone was working with the same end in mind, but they were working in different and essential *roles*. One group figured out how to turn the spaceship around. Another group fixed the oxygen problem. Another dealt with the reentry calculations, and the spare crew did whatever it took to complete the mission.

6. Once the immediate issue and burning imperative had been resolved, NASA embedded rigorous practices to minimize risks and maximize performance as a step in the *evolution* of standard operating procedure going forward.

Even though you're unlikely to jump into a situation exactly like the Apollo 13 breakdown, in today's environment almost all leadership transitions are "hot landings," where you must hit the ground running to have a chance of success.

The 100-Day Action Plan

The 100-Day Action Plan, as detailed in the chapters in this book, outlines a process for leaders to converge into an organization and then evolve the organization with a co-created and shared burning imperative that will lead to better results faster.

Get a Head Start

1. Position yourself for success. Get the job. Make sure it is right for you. Avoid common land mines.
2. Leverage the fuzzy front end. The job starts when you accept the offer.

Manage the Message

3. Take control of day one. Make a powerful first impression. Confirm your entry message.
4. Evolve the culture. Leverage diversity.
5. Manage communication, especially digitally with your remote team.

Set Direction, and Build the Team

6. Pivot to strategy. Co-create the burning imperative by Day 30.
7. Drive operational accountability. Embed milestone management by Day 45.
8. Select early wins by Day 60 to deliver within 6 months.
9. Build a high-performing team. Realign, acquire, enable, mentor by Day 70.

Sustain Momentum, and Deliver Results

10. Advance and adjust your own leadership, practices, team, and culture by Day 100.

Culture

In many respects, leadership is an exercise in building a culture. However you define it, culture is the glue that holds organizations together.

This book focuses on pivotal events such as joining a new organization, leading a turnaround, or merging teams as opportunities to accelerate culture change and results. These transitions are about creating and bridging gaps: between leaders and their new teams, between aspirational states and current realities.

You must understand and intentionally nurture culture throughout your onboarding, especially when you:

- Prepare for interviews (to answer cultural fit questions)
- Complete your due diligence (to mitigate organizational, role, and personal land mines)
- Choose your onboarding approach (by crossing the business's need for change with the culture's readiness for change and your own risk profile)
- Converge into the organizational culture
- Evolve the organization's culture

Cultural elements are particularly critical to get right in a post-merger integration. Too little effort is paid to culture during integrations, 70 percent of those surveyed in the 2009 Post Merger Integration Conference acknowledged, with 92 percent claiming that greater cultural understanding would have substantially benefited mergers. And respondents assigned blame for cultural difficulties to "poor leadership of the integration effort" as opposed to "wrong choice of target" by a factor of five to one![6] The message: Culture is critical, integration is where the rubber meets the road, and leadership matters when combining cultures.

Communication—It Starts with Listening

The other thread that runs through this book is communication. Because everything communicates, guidance on communication belongs in every step and every chapter.

One idea that jars some people is the recommendation to craft the going-in headline message before Day One. Leaders wonder how they can do that before they've completed their listening tour. You will have learned a fair amount about the organization, its priorities, and its people during your interview and due diligence stages. If you know enough to have been offered and accepted the job, you know enough to craft an initial message. Take your best current thinking, craft a hypothetical message, and use that to direct your future learning.

With that as background, here are the steps of the 100-Day Action Plan and the chapters of this book.

---

[6] Clay Deutsch and Andy West, 2010, *Perspectives on Merger Integration*, McKinsey, June.

FIGURE 0.4   The New Leader's 100-Day Action Plan

Converge					Pivot		Evolve		
Day One				30	45	60	70		100
Position Yourself for success	Leverage the Fuzzy Front End	Take control of Day One	Lay your Leadership Foundation	Co-create Burning Imperative	Embed Milestone Management	Invest in Early Wins	Realign Team	Adjust and Advance	

Chapter 1: Position Yourself for Success: Get the Job. Make Sure It Is Right for You. Avoid Common Land Mines.

Leadership is personal. The greater the congruence between your own preferences across behaviors, relationships, attitudes, values, and environment and the new culture you enter or create, the stronger those connections and your organizing concept will be. Note that while you're converging, resist sharing your ideas until you've earned that right. Let your headline message guide your questions, communicating what you care about without you ever saying it.

Great leaders live their messages—not because they can but because they must. "Here I stand, I can do no other."[7] Knowing your own strengths and cultural preferences will help you better create career options that are a true fit for you, will allow you to do a better job positioning yourself in interviews (selling before you buy), and will help you do a thorough due diligence to mitigate risks.

Along the way, be sure to take into account evolving changes in sensibilities to work–life balance, health and well-being, relationships, diversity, equity and inclusion, and the challenges of leading teams and building culture in remote and virtual environments.

Chapter 2: The Job Starts When You Accept the Offer: Leverage the Fuzzy Front End.

At this point you've made the choice—but you haven't started yet. There's a temptation to take a deep breath and relax. Don't do that.

---

[7] Attributed to Martin Luther at the Diet of Worms, 1521, when asked to recant his earlier writings.

FIGURE 0.5 ACES

Context	Ready to change	Not ready to change
Strong need to change	Converge and Evolve Quickly	Shock
Less need to change now	Assimilate	Converge and Evolve Slowly
Culture	Ready to change	Not ready to change

What you do next, what you do before Day One, can make all the difference. So choose the right approach for your situation, draft a plan, and get a head start.

Figure 0.5 shows a few dimensions to choosing the right approach.

First, the approach is different if you're joining a new company, getting promoted or transferred from within, running a private equity–owned business, crossing international boundaries, or merging teams. Second, the business context and the culture's readiness for change will inform your choice around whether to assimilate in slowly, converge and evolve, or shock the organization with sudden changes.

Armed with the choice about your overall approach and what you'll need to do differently as a leader in this situation, you're ready to create a 100-day plan targeting the most important stakeholders up, across, and down—both inside the organization and out, laying out your best current thinking around your message, what you're going to do between now and Day One, on Day One, and over your first 100 days and beyond. These efforts include prestart conversations to jump-start your important relationships and learning, as well as focus on various aspects of your personal setup.

MasterCard's Ajay Banga managed his fuzzy front end and early days particularly well. He leveraged the time after he had been announced as CEO but before he started by casually, but pointedly, interacting with key stakeholders with a simple introduction: "Hi, I'm Ajay. Tell me about yourself."[8]

---

[8] George Bradt, 2011, "Why Preparing in Advance Is Priceless: How MasterCard CEO Ajay Banga Planned Ahead for His New Leadership Role," *Forbes*, February 23.

Chapter 3: Take Control of Day One: Make a Powerful First Impression. Confirm Your Entry Message.

Everything is magnified on Day One, whether you are joining a new company, entering a private equity portfolio, or announcing an acquisition. Everyone is looking for hints about what you think and what you're going to do. People's only real question is, "What does this mean for me?"

This is why it's so important to seed your message by paying particular attention to all the signs, symbols, and stories you deploy and the order in which you deploy them. Make sure that people are seeing and hearing things that will lead them to believe and feel what you want them to believe and feel about you and about themselves in relation to the future of the organization.

Sierra Club's executive director Michael Brune did a particularly good job of managing his Day One. He thought through his message in advance and then communicated it live, face-to-face, and via social media on his first day so that everyone would know what was on his mind. He smartly used several communication methods to reach a wide range of people in their own preferred way of communication.[9]

Chapter 4: Evolve the Culture. Leverage Diversity.

Leaders inspire, enable, and empower others to do their absolute best together to realize a meaningful and rewarding shared purpose.

Think in terms of why people follow you, what you do, and how you help those following you. Since leadership, culture, and communications are inextricably linked, this chapter will tackle all three as you lay the foundation of your leadership to bridge from your early days to building tactical capacity into your team.

Diversity, equity, and inclusion (DE&I) have changed from the right things to do to essential to the future survival of your organization. DE&I is not a goal. It's not a theory. It's time to make it real and concrete.

---

[9] George Bradt, 2011, "Powerful First Impressions: Michael Brune's Day One at the Sierra Club," *Forbes*, March 2.

Chapter 5: Manage Communication, Especially Digitally with Your Remote Team.

The prescription for communication during the time between Day One and cocreating a burning imperative is counterintuitive and stressful for new leaders following this program. The fundamental approach is to converge and evolve. And the time before cocreating a burning imperative is all about converging. This means you can't launch your full-blown communication efforts yet. You can't stand up and tell people your new ideas. If you do, they are your ideas, not invented here and not the team's ideas.

So before you pivot, refine your best current thinking about communication, and begin to establish your leadership and transform the culture by your questions, your active listening, and your behaviors and not just by what you say. Then, it all changes as you pivot.

Remote work is here to stay. Embrace that fact and learn to lead people in the new trust-based ways remote work requires. We'll share with you ways to do that effectively.

Chapter 6: Pivot to Strategy: Co-create the Burning Imperative by Day 30.

The burning imperative is a sharply defined, intensely shared, and purposefully urgent understanding from the team members of what they are "supposed to do now" and how this works with the larger aspirations of the team and the organization. Mission, vision, values, goals, objectives, and action-based strategies are key components of the burning imperative. The essence of the imperative is articulated in the rallying cry that everyone understands and can act on. Co-create this with the team to get buy-in early, even if your best current thinking is only 80 percent right. You, and your team, will adjust and improve along the way. Get this in place in your first 30 days!

There are four primary areas of focus for company competitiveness: design, produce, deliver, and service (Figure 0.6). Most organizations do all four to one degree or another in addition to marketing and selling, which all must do. Align all around which is your core focus and primary differentiator, with approaches around operations, organization, leadership, and culture flowing from that.

FIGURE 0.6   Core Focus

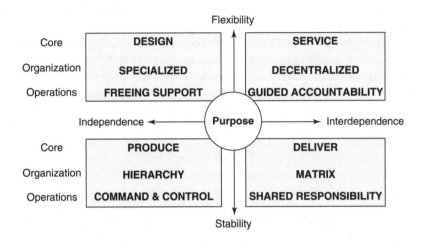

Chapter 7: Drive Operational Accountability: Embed Milestone Management by Day 45.

The real test of a high-performing team's tactical capacity lies in their ability to deliver results. Critical to that success are the operational practices that clarify ownership, decision rights, and information flows, identifying execution risk so the team can collaborate and get back on track.[10]

Royal Caribbean's former CEO Richard Fain explains it this way:

If you don't establish early on key milestones—long-term milestones rather than the short-term milestones—you get caught in the "next week" syndrome. . . . Everybody says, "We're going to know so much more next week or the week after". . . . so the focus shifts to next week or the week after and we all desperately wait for that period. Meanwhile the longer-term milestone goes by the wayside.[11]

---

[10] Gary L. Neilson, Karla L. Martin, and Elizabeth Powers, 2008, "The Secrets to Successful Strategy Execution," *Harvard Business Review*, June.

[11] George Bradt, 2011, "Royal Caribbean's CEO Exemplifies How to Leverage Milestones," *Forbes*, March 23.

Chapter 8: Select Early Wins by Day 60 to Deliver Results Within 6 Months.

Early wins are all about credibility and confidence. People have more faith in people who have delivered. You want team members to have confidence in you, in themselves, and in the plan for change that has emerged. You want your boss to have confidence in you. Early wins fuel that confidence. To that end, jump-start potential early wins by Day 60, and overinvest to deliver them by the end of your first 6 months—as a team!

Chapter 9: Build a High-Performing Team: Realign, Acquire, Enable, and Mentor by Day 70.

Make your organization stronger by acquiring, developing, encouraging, planning, and transitioning talent:

Acquire: Recruit, attract, and onboard the right people with the right talent.

Develop: Assess and build skills, knowledge, experience, and craft.

Encourage: Direct, support, recognize, and reward.

Plan: Monitor, assess, and plan career moves over time.

Transition: Migrate to different roles as appropriate.

Start by defining the right structure and roles to execute on your mission. Turnarounds, transformations, and M&A integrations may require different roles to address the added complexity in those types of transitions. Be specific about talent, knowledge, skill, experience, and craft requirements in each key role, and then match them with the right people.

Pay attention to differences. The world needs three types of leaders: scientific leaders who influence knowledge, artistic leaders who influence feelings, and interpersonal leaders who influence actions. These three are not always mutually exclusive. Jump-start your team by getting the right people in the right roles with the right support to build the team.

Chapter 10: Adjust and Advance Your Own Leadership, People, Practices, and Culture by Day 100.

By the 100-day mark you will have put a plan in place, leveraged the time before Day One to learn quickly, developed solid relationships with key stakeholders, engaged the culture, and made a strong early impression by delivering a clear message to your new audiences (up, down, and across). Your team will be in place, energized by its co-created burning imperative, and will have established milestone management practices to drive accountability and have early wins in sight.

So, what's next? Move forward with the process of continual evolution in four key areas:

1. **Leadership:** The 100-day mark is a good moment to perform a self-assessment and gain feedback on your own leadership so that you can determine *what* you should keep, stop, and start doing—and *how*—to be even more effective with your team and the organization as a whole.

2. **People:** Decide how you are going to evolve your people and related processes in line with changing circumstances.

3. **Practices:** From there, it is an opportune time to decide how you are going to evolve your practices to capitalize on changing circumstances. You should focus on practices that relate to people, plans, performance tracking, and program management.

4. **Culture:** Finally, after 100 days, your insights on the culture will be sharper than when you started. Also, you will be clearer about how you want to *evolve the culture*. Now is the time to zero in on the biggest gaps and implement a plan to create and maintain the winning culture that will become your greatest competitive advantage.

By evolving your own leadership, practices, and culture, you will be setting yourself and your team up to deliver better results faster and sustainably over time.

Walmart's CEO Mike Duke knows that we are all new leaders all the time. That's why organizational change management is an ongoing part of his life. When Walmart's merchandising failed to deliver the expected results over the 2010 holiday season, Mike replaced his head merchandiser and completely revamped their holiday merchandising approach in time to announce the changes in their next quarter's earnings call.[12]

Chapter 11: Manage Your New Board.

Boards of directors provide oversight, approve the most material decisions, and advise, whereas management has accountability for strategy, operations, and the organization. As CEO, follow Deloitte's Seven Steps:

1. CEOs, it's really up to you—Take an active role in board management.

2. Be fearlessly transparent—Be open and humble.

3. Take advantage of tension—Grow through debate.

4. Facilitate the board experience, not just the board meeting—Build relationships over time.

5. Curate information, and then curate it again—Give enough, but not too much information.

6. To chair or not to chair? Think about it very carefully—Choose your level of influence.

7. Say your piece on board composition—Build the right board over time.

The Board Two-Step can help a lot here. Step 1: Seek their input. Then go away so they can talk amongst themselves, with others, or give you off-the-record perspective. Step 2: Taking into account their input, and encouraging debate, seek their approval to your recommended path forward.

Invest in all board relationships, particularly with the lead director, who will help you manage the board.

---

[12] George Bradt, 2011, "Walmart CEO Mike Duke Shifts Approach," *Forbes*, March 1.

Chapter 12: Lead Through Mergers and Acquisitions.

Those leading through a merger, acquisition, or the like do so to accelerate value creation. They look for revenues to double or more on the way to returning many multiples of their initial investments. Maybe you're driving or leading the investment. Maybe you're leading the business itself or playing a supporting role. In any case, you need a leadership playbook for the merger or acquisition. Our playbook has 14 steps:

1. Start with the **investment case**—the heart of your playbook.

2. Do **the deal** in a way that reduces your risk of being part of the 83 percent of mergers and acquisitions (M&A) that fail to deliver the desired results.

3. Do your **due diligence** on the key ingredients for success.

4. Start setting up **cultural integration** well before the deal closes to help your new people become valued participants in the new organization.

5. Choose your **key leaders** before the close or kick-off: Share the vision and get them aligned—including starting up an integration office.

6. **Plan** for success with your key leaders, focusing on customers, people, and costs—in that order.

7. Manage the **politics**: What current and new leaders need to know organizationally and personally.

8. Avoid early land mines with a well-crafted **announcement cascade**.

9. Get the right **people** in the right roles much faster than you think you should.

10. Deploy the fundamentals of **change management** to inspire, enable, and empower others.

11. Leverage **cost-cutting** as an enabler while jump-starting your operational, executional, and financial processes.

12. Keep going with ongoing **communication** both ways. Because your communication campaign never ends, you can never overcommunicate.

13. **Adjust** along the way: How to recognize, prioritize, and make the right moves to realize the investment case.

14. Prepare for the **next chapter,** successfully acquiring others—or a sale or liquidity event.

Chapter 13: Lead a Turnaround.

Whatever the impetus for your turnaround or transformation, you should be excited about the possibilities—and concerned about the risks. Seventy percent of transformations fail to deliver desired results.[13] This is why you need to jump-shift your own game, accelerate success, and mitigate risks all at the same time.

As you step into the leadership role of a turnaround, be aware of these six critical success mindsets:

1. Call it and communicate it.

2. Understand and align expectations.

3. Move quickly and decisively.

4. Over-communicate.

5. Over-invest for innovation.

6. Enter humble. Leave confident.

Then follow these five steps:

1. **Define catalysts.** Assess the changes in the situation and be clear what's triggering the need for change.

2. **Reset strategy for winning.** Agree on the core focus of the enterprise, its mission, vision, goals, objectives, a new overarching strategy, strategic priorities, enablers, capabilities, and culture. Understand and plan for the degree of change the new strategy represents.

3. **Reorganize for success.** Create a new organizational structure and future capability plan in line with your new strategy. New

---

[13] Rajiv Chandran et al., 2015, "Ascending to the C-Suite," *McKinsey Insights*, April.

roles (permanent and temporary) are likely needed to jump-start and sustain the effort.

4. **Intensify operating cadence.** Implement a more intense management cadence to track and manage your priorities annually, programs monthly, and projects weekly as appropriate.

5. **Embed learning and communication.** Deploy a purpose-driven learning and communication effort in line with your new operating flow and management cadence to lead change over an 18-month timeline.

Chapter 14: Lead Through a Crisis: A 100-Hour Action Plan.

Leading through a crisis is about inspiring, enabling, and empowering others to get things vaguely right quickly, and then adapt along the way—with clarity around direction, leadership, and roles.

This plays out in three steps of a disciplined iteration in line with an organization's overall purpose:

1. **Prepare in advance:** The better you have anticipated possible scenarios, the more prepared you are, the more confidence you will have when crises strike.

2. **React to events:** The reason you prepared is so that you all can react quickly and flexibility to the situation you face. Don't overthink this. Do what you prepared to do.

3. **Bridge the gaps:** In a crisis, there is inevitably a gap between the desired and current state. Rectify that by bridging those gaps in the:

   • Situation—implementing a response to the current crisis

   • Response—improving capabilities to respond to future crises

   • Prevention—reducing the risk of future crises happening in the first place

Along the way, keep the ultimate purpose in mind. It needs to inform and frame everything you do over the short-, mid-, and long-term as you lead through a crisis instead of merely out of a crisis.

Crises change your organization. Be sure the choices you make during crises change you in ways that move you toward your purpose and desired culture and not away from your core vision and values.

Make This Book Work for You

By now you should be aware that there may be a better way to manage transitions than just showing up on Day One or charging into your promotion announcement or newly merged team and doing what *they* tell you to do. Similarly, there may be a better way for you to tackle this book than just starting on page one and reading straight through until you lose steam.

This is designed to be a flexible playbook split into three parts: (1) the book itself; (2) downloadable and editable tools; and (3) more extensive notes and content on primegenesis.com/tools. You might want to start with the 100-Day worksheet (Tool 2.1) at the end of Chapter 2 or the sample 100-day worksheets on the website. You might prefer to begin with the chapter summaries or to read straight through the main body of the book. Use the book's elements in the way that works best for you.

People often tell us, "This is just common sense. But I like the way you've structured it." (One person said, "You brought together all of the critical thinking sessions I had with myself in the shower every morning before work!" We'll let you imagine that in your own way.)

Do be aware of our bias to push you to do things faster than others would expect. The 100-Day Plan is based on the needs of new leaders moving into critical situations who must meet or beat high expectations fast, but it may not be appropriate for your situation without some customization. We present to you options and choices. You are in charge. We wish you success in your new leadership role. We hope this book will help you and your team deliver better results faster than anyone thought possible!

The most up-to-date, full, editable versions of all tools are downloadable at primegenesis.com/tools.

Chapter 1

Chapter 2

Chapter 3

PART I

The New Leader's 100-Day Action Plan

Position Yourself for Success

GET THE JOB. MAKE SURE IT IS RIGHT FOR YOU. AVOID COMMON LAND MINES.

Converge							Evolve		
		Day One		30	45	60	70		100
Position Yourself for success	Leverage the Fuzzy Front End	Take control of Day One	Lay your Leadership Foundation	Co-create Burning Imperative	Embed Milestone Management	Invest in Early Wins	Realign Team		Adjust and Advance

As discussed in the executive summary, the four main ideas in this book are:

1. Get a head start.
2. Manage the message.
3. Set direction. Build the team.
4. Sustain momentum. Deliver results.

As you start to position yourself for success, know that leadership is personal. Your message is the key that unlocks personal connections. The greater the congruence between your own preferences across behaviors, relationships, attitudes, values, and environment

(BRAVE) and the new culture you enter or create, the stronger those connections will be. This is why the best messages aren't crafted—they emerge. This is why great leaders live their messages not because they can, but because they must. "Here I stand; I can do no other."[1]

An organization's culture is the collective character of its members. Understanding your own BRAVE preferences helps you understand and explain your character. This will help you figure out your fit with potential new organizations and how you would influence and impact their cultures.

Along the way, be sure to take into account your perspective on evolving topics such as work environment (remote versus in-person), work–life balance, diversity, equity and inclusion, and the integration of new generations into the workforce and the leadership ranks.

Take time to stop and figure out which of those are more important to you and which are less important and how your preferences and character have evolved over time. Be clear on what are the mandatory overlaps between your BRAVE preferences and the culture of an organization in which you can thrive.

Knowing your strengths, motivations, and preferences will help you create career options that are a fit for you, will allow you to effectively position yourself in interviews (sell before you buy), and will guide you to mitigate risks through targeted due diligence.

"I wish I'd read this chapter before I accepted that job!" We hear that a lot.

Culture First

In many respects, leadership is an exercise in building culture. However, you define it, culture is the glue that holds organizations together. Culture is often impacted by pivotal events, such as a new leader joining an organization, combining organizations post–M&A, or a significant external event. These moments present opportunities to accelerate culture change and deliver better results. Culture change

---

[1] Attributed to Martin Luther at the Diet of Worms, 1521, when asked to recant his earlier writings.

is about bridging the gap between the current state and the desired state which better enables a team to achieve the organization's mission and goals.

The greater the cultural differences, the more difficult the adaptation or change will be. There's real power in understanding the most important cultural differences and then building a plan to bridge those gaps over time.

Some define culture simply as "the way we do things around here." Others conduct complex analyses to define it more scientifically. Instead, blend both schools of thought into an implementable approach that defines culture as an organization's behaviors, relationships, attitudes, values, and the environment (BRAVE). The BRAVE framework is relatively easy to apply yet offers a relatively robust way to identify, engage, and change a culture. It makes culture real, tangible, identifiable, and easy to talk about.

It's helpful to tackle the BRAVE components from the outside in with five questions, as shown in Table 1.1.

When evaluating each element of culture, think of it on a sliding scale (say 1–5) rather than in absolute terms. The specific dimensions within each cultural component may vary from situation to situation.

You may find the components and dimensions in Tool 1.1 helpful.

The impact on culture is an essential consideration in almost every action, tool, and communication you will deploy in your first 100 days and beyond. Many organizational experts argue that culture is the only truly sustainable competitive advantage for an organization over the long run.

Table 1.1
BRAVE Framework

Component	Question	Essence
Environment	Where to play?	(Context)
Values	What matters and why?	(Purpose)
Attitudes	How to win?	(Choices)
Relationships	How to connect?	(Influence)
Behaviors	What Impact?	(Implementation)

NOTE ON CULTURE

You must consider culture throughout your 100-Day Plan, especially when you:

- Prepare for interviews (to answer cultural fit questions)
- Complete your due diligence (to mitigate organizational, role, and personal land mines)
- Choose your onboarding approach (by comparing the business's need for change to the culture's readiness for change)
- Converge into the organization's culture
- Evolve the organization's culture

In short, consider the cultural impact of every choice you make, or don't make in your first 100 days . . . and beyond. Forever.

See Tool 1A.10 at primegenesis.com/tools for a discussion of culture across all the steps of onboarding. (Same material as in the book, just compiled into a single tool on BRAVE culture.)

Sell Before You Buy

Securing a new leadership position usually requires interviews. You can ace any interview if you remember three things during the process:

Thing 1: You cannot turn down or accept a job offer that you have not received.

Thing 2: There are only three fundamental interview questions— ever.

Thing 3: There are only three fundamental interview answers— ever.

Thing 1

Before you accept a job, you must first get an offer. Then, and only then, can you decide whether you should accept it. Do not do these steps out of order. Your initial focus should be on getting the job offer.

If you start to imagine or assume you have the job before you have the offer, you have diverted some of your energy away from reality and are wasting your time. Once you have received the offer, your approach should change.

Everything you do in the interview process should be designed to get someone else to offer you the job. This includes not only your answers to their questions but also your questions to them. At this stage in the process, your questions are not about helping you decide whether you want the job. They are about helping them decide to offer it to you. Sell yourself first. Secure the offer. Then, after you have the offer, and only then, figure out whether it's right for you.

Thing 2

There are only three interview questions. Every question you've ever been asked, and every question you've ever asked in any interview, is a subset of one of these three fundamental questions:

1. Can you do the job?
2. Will you love the job?
3. Can we tolerate working with you?

Those three questions asked in a more traditional way are:

1. What are your strengths?
2. Will you be motivated to do the job?
3. Are you a fit?

That's it: strengths, motivation, fit. The questions may be asked in different ways, but every question, however worded, is just a variation on one of these. As each question comes, it is your task to determine which of the three is really being asked.

Thing 3

Because there are only three fundamental interview questions, there are only three fundamental interview answers.

Every answer you give in an interview should be a subset of these three answers:

1. My strengths are a match for this job.
2. My motivations are a match for this job.
3. I am a good fit for this organization.

That's it. Those three. Your answers to questions will be more elaborate, but your answers should always be dressed-up versions of one of the three.

Because there are only three interview questions and only three interview answers, all you have to do is to prepare three answers in advance and recognize what question you are being asked. Then you are ready to ace any interview.

The bad news is that it is going to be a lot more work than you might think to prepare these answers in advance of each interview. Interviews are exercises in solution selling. They are not about you. They are about your interviewers—their needs, their problems. You are the solution. Think of the interview process as a chance for you to show your ability to see, hear, and solve the organization and interviewer's problem.

If interviewers know what they are doing, they will be looking beyond a narrowly defined problem (and solution) and for technical expertise across a broader set of criteria: strengths, motivations, and fit. When they don't really know what they're doing, they can be brought around to seeing things the right way. Still, in every case the solution must be presented from their perspective. Thoughtful preparation can be the deciding factor between a yes and a no. This is tricky stuff, but it is worth the investment of time.

Question 1: Can you do the job? Or more likely, what are your strengths? (Strengths)

Answer 1: Prepare three situation/action/results examples that highlight your strengths in the areas most important over the short term and long term to the people interviewing you. Refer not only to what you've learned from the position description, the recruiter, and those interviewing you but also consider recent events (competitors' moves, marketplace changes, economic policies, global shifts, political changes, crises, and others) that may indicate a change in the requirements for the job.

Meanwhile, it's counterintuitive, but strive to be the 90–10 loser. Your goal is not to get every and any job offer. Your goal should be to get the right job. Instead of being generally right for 60 percent of the jobs, be wrong for 90 percent of them, and look to be the "must have" candidate for 10 percent of them. If you answer your interview questions by focusing on strength, motivation, and fit, you will land a job based on your innate talent, learned knowledge, practiced skills, hard-won experience, and cultural fit. Those are the jobs where you will truly excel.

> Question 2: Will you love the job? Or more likely, what are you looking to do? (Motivation)
>
> Answer 2: Discuss how the role you are applying for matches what matters most to you. Smart interviewers' first question will be "Why would you want this job?" They'll know instantly whether you care more about doing good for others, doing things you're good at, or doing good for yourself. Be sure to tie your responses clearly to what will make a difference for the person, and the organization interviewing you.
>
> Question 3: Can I tolerate working with you? Or more likely, what sort of people do you like to work with? (Fit)
>
> Answer 3: Discuss how your preferences across behaviors, relationships, attitudes, values, and the environment match the organization's culture on those dimensions.

In some cases, where role specifications are not as clear as you'd like (they often are not), it can be useful to imagine that you are interviewing for a job where a new leader and a new team are being put together to solve a specific problem or to address a specific need or goal. To become the winning candidate, you may need to act as a management consultant, helping the decision-makers and team members get a better sense of what the problems, or needs, really are, and then conveying confidence that under your supervision the right things will get done.

Note you'll find more discussion about the questions behind the questions at primegenesis.com/tools.

HOT TIP

Everything is part of the interview: You won't go too far wrong if you imagine that everything you do and say is being videotaped to be shown to the final decision-maker. This is why you must use every part of every interaction with everybody in the organization as an opportunity to reinforce your strengths, motivation, and fit. Until you've been offered a job, it's all about getting the offer.

The Seven Deadly Land Mines

The first 100 days in your new role will be rife with land mines; just like the real thing, they are usually hidden and are often undetected until it is too late. Being aware that land mines exist and learning how to anticipate them will limit their devastating potential. Learning how to deactivate them safely will help you sail straight through to success.

Land mines will always exist but they are most easily hidden from you leading up to and through your first 100 days. Know that you must always be mitigating all of these land mines during and well beyond your transition.

WARNING!

What follows discusses these land mines one by one, but they frequently come in multiples and often interact with each other. Exposure to one risk heightens others, and failure has a way of gaining its own terrible and often unstoppable momentum.

Additionally, land mines are particularly challenging to diagnose when an interview process is more remote than in person, where the organization's external environment is more changing than stable, or when there are disconnects across the interviewing team. Be sure to gather multiple perspectives both inside and outside the company when these kinds of circumstances exist.

Land Mine 1: Organization

The lack of a clear, concise, differentiating, and winning strategy creates an organizational land mine.

You do not want to get on a ship that is doomed to sink. Some people thrive on this risk and want to be part of the turnaround. It is one thing to be a turnaround expert going into an organization that knows it needs to make significant changes fast. It is a recipe for disaster if you are not a turnaround expert and you're going into an organization that needs those skills but doesn't actually realize it.

Best time to mitigate/deactivate: Before accepting the job.

Deactivation method: Ask tough questions early and often to internal and external sources.

Land Mine 2: Role

If expectations, resources, or key stakeholders are not aligned, you will encounter a role land mine. Often, new leaders step into jobs that are virtually impossible from the start because the expectations are unrealistic or cannot be delivered for whatever reason.

The role land mine can be particularly common when a leader is entering a role that is new to the organization and "sits between" existing functions and departments.

Best time to mitigate/deactivate: Before accepting the job.

Deactivation method: Listen for inconsistencies or uncertainty around your (1) role and responsibilities, (2) deliverables, (3) timetable, (4) decision-making authority, (5) interactions, and (6) access to essential resources.

Land Mine 3: Personal

Personal land mines are the ones that you bring to the new job. They are activated when significant gaps exist in your strengths, motivation, or fit for the job. Often executives assume that their strengths are well matched to a particular role, when in fact they are not. Assumptions about strengths usually are based on prior success without a true in-depth assessment of the match between strengths and the particular situation. Although a new job may sound like your former job, there will be a whole new range of dynamics that may require significantly different skill sets. By missing this factor, leaders often fail to realize that they may not possess certain strengths that are essential for success in the new role. But this is not you.

Best time to mitigate/deactivate: Before accepting the job.

Deactivation method: Ask yourself the tough questions about whether you really have the strengths, motivation, and fit required for success for this particular role.

Land Mine 4: Relationships

If you fail to identify, establish, or maintain key relationships up, across, or down, you will encounter relationship land mines. (There may be clusters of these, and they can set each other off in succession; watch out!) These key relationships are those that have a stake in or can impact your success. These stakeholders can be found up, down, or across the organization from you.

When you miss the needs or agendas of other key stakeholders or outside influencers, there is a good chance that some impact will be felt. The problem is you won't necessarily know that this has started to happen, but it can get a life and a momentum of its own outside of your presence or even awareness. If you lend an insufficient or ineffective effort to building a productive teamwork environment with direct reports, land mines are often the result. If expectations of up stakeholders are not clearly understood, go unchecked, or frequently change, this is certainly dangerous territory for land mines. Finally, poor preparation and communication follow-through are often key culprits in activating these land mines.

Relationship land mines catch many executives completely unaware. These are especially tricky because sometimes the results of stepping on one do not show up for months, or longer. What is worse, you can get caught by these land mines just by pure neglect of a key stakeholder or someone who you didn't even know should be a key stakeholder: "I was just too busy to reach out to her." "He has a role in all this? He's just the head of investor relations!"

Relationship risks are particularly severe for people who are brought in as change agents. Often those people come in with a hero mentality, thinking they are the organization's savior. This is not necessarily a problem and sometimes they're right. The problem occurs when new leaders *act* as if they are saviors. Nobody wants to see that, especially those who have been part of the situation that needs saving. Don't be a savior. Be a team leader. History is littered with many dead heroes who never made it home.

Best time to mitigate/deactivate: Between acceptance and start. Ongoing.

Deactivation method: Activate a 360-relationship compass and use it to help guide you to potential challenges and land mines. Continually evaluate your stakeholder list up, down, and across to ensure you're not missing anyone critical to your success. Often your boss, human resources, close colleagues, and even recruiters can provide insight on anyone you may be missing. Don't be afraid to ask.

Land Mine 5: Learning

Fail to grasp key information in any of the 6 Cs (customers, collaborators, culture, capabilities, competitors, conditions) and you have effectively created learning land mines. Executives often miss the importance of certain Cs or diminish the importance of one or more. If you don't have a learning plan in place for each and every C, the likelihood of undetected land mines greatly increases.

If you don't know what you need to know or—worse yet—don't know what you don't know, then land mines will surely be plentiful. So what do you need to know? At the very least, you need to know critical information about each of the 6 Cs, especially about the real value chain of your business. If you use our guidelines for your 6 Cs analysis, the information you gather will significantly diminish the risk of learning land mines.

Learning is essential. Being perceived as wanting to learn is almost as important as learning itself. You have heard it before: "Seek first to understand,"[2] "Don't come in with the answer,"[3] "Wisdom begins in wonder."[4] You hear it repeatedly in many different ways because it is proven advice. Heed it. You need to learn and you'll want to be perceived as being hungry to learn, not only about the "hard

---

[2] Stephen Covey, 1989, *The 7 Habits of Highly Effective People*, New York: Simon & Schuster.
[3] Michael Watkins, 2003, *The First 90 Days*, Boston: Harvard Business School Press.
[4] Attributed to Socrates.

facts" of the business, but also about cultural factors such as decision-making processes, communication styles, and the like.

Best time to mitigate/deactivate: Between acceptance and start. Ongoing, especially during first 60 days.

Deactivation method: Activate an ongoing learning campaign, with inputs from multiple sources, to thoroughly master the 6 Cs.

Land Mine 6: Delivery

In the end, it boils down to delivery. It's not what you do; it's the results you deliver. If you deliver, the organization can tolerate many other faults. If you are leading a team, you cannot deliver if the team does not deliver. At the end of your first 100 days, the most dangerous land mine is failing to build a high-performing team fast enough to deliver the expected results in the expected time frame.

Best time to mitigate/deactivate: First 100 days.

Deactivation method: Identify clear and genuine winning deliverables and timetables. Validate with key stakeholders. Empower and execute with the team.

Land Mine 7: Adjustment

You can do everything correctly to this point, but if you do not see or react to the inevitable situational changes, then new land mines will certainly be created. The act of planning and managing is not a static exercise. You must be keenly aware of the fluid dynamics of your team's situation. Missing the need to survey the environment constantly and adjust accordingly is just like a skipper setting sail for a destination and never adjusting his or her sails for the ever-changing seas and weather conditions.

Things change, and you and your team need to change when they do. Sometimes you can get away with minor adjustments. Sometimes a complete restart is required. The risk lies in not seeing the need to change, in not understanding how to change effectively, or in being too slow to react to the changes you do see.

Best time to mitigate/deactivate: As appropriate.

Deactivation method: Monitor business conditions, results, and organization changes actively. Gain stakeholder feedback. Understand the causes and implications of change. Course correct quickly.

You've got a choice. You can leverage our suggested approach to uncover and help you assess and mitigate those risks. Or you can send us an e-mail later saying, "I wish I'd read this chapter before I accepted that job!" You won't be alone.

Do Your Due Diligence Before You Accept the Job Offer

Should I take this job? To know the answer to that question, you need to make an informed assessment of the degree of risk. Almost nobody wants to do due diligence. Almost nobody likes to do due diligence. Almost nobody knows how to do due diligence well. It's as though people don't want to do anything to spoil the moment of getting a job offer. Ignorance can be bliss—until the things you didn't see show up and conk you on the head.

At the core, due diligence is an exercise in collecting and analyzing information from multiple sources to understand the risk inherent in a decision. As with just about everything discussed in this book, a carefully thought out and methodical approach will help. Don't be afraid of any negative news you learn. At worst, it might provide a strong indication that this is not the job for you, and at best it will help you get an accurate picture of the challenge at hand before you start the job. In either scenario, you are better off for knowing before you accept the job.

Mitigate Risk Before You Accept a Job

To avoid trying to boil the ocean, you've got to focus your risk assessment on exploring the few most important areas. Before accepting a job, you must gather information in the following areas to answer three fundamental questions around organization, role, and personal risks.

Start by doing a complete 6 Cs situation assessment using Tool 1.2, and then pull it all together with a SWOT analysis.

Once you've gathered your information, you've analyzed it, and thought about it, now what do you do? Categorize the risk as low, manageable, mission crippling, or insurmountable and then take appropriate action. Use Tool 1.4 for this exercise.

Summary and Implications

- **Culture**—Understand your own cultural preferences and strengths in the context of potential job opportunities.

- **Sell before you buy**—Get the offer first. You cannot turn down an offer you have not received. So sell before you buy, positioning your strengths, motivation, and fit in the context of the interviewing organization's needs.

- **Due diligence**—Do a real due diligence before accepting; understand the level of risk you face across the seven deadly land mines (organization, role, personal, relationship, learning, delivery, and adjustment).

- **Manage risk**—Manage that risk appropriately with the help you need.

QUESTIONS YOU SHOULD ASK YOURSELF

Culture—Am I clear on my cultural preferences? How do my preferences compare with the organization's culture?

Sell before you buy—Do I have examples to support my answers to the three interview questions?

Due diligence—Have I done sufficient due diligence with a sufficiently broad array of inputs?

Manage risk—Do I understand the risks and have I thought through my approach to manage those risks?

Summary

Note the most up-to-date, full, editable versions of all tools are downloadable at primegenesis.com/tools.

TOOL 1.1

BRAVE Culture Assessment/ Preference

For each of the following components, estimate on a scale of 1–5, where 1 indicates the text in the left column completely describes the preference and 5 indicates the text in the right column completely describes the preference. Score your preferences and the organization's preferences. Add and score other subcomponents as you identify them. Identify the most important gaps and determine whether or how the gaps can be bridged.

Environment—Where play

WORKPLACE
Remote, virtual, open, informal   1–2–3–4–5 In-person, closed, formal
WORK–LIFE BALANCE
Health and wellness first   1–2–3–4–5 Near-term productivity first
ENABLERS
Human/interpersonal/societal   1–2–3–4–5 Technical/mechanical/scientific

Values—What matters and why

FOCUS
Do good for others/ESG   1–2–3–4–5 Do good for selves/what good at
RISK APPETITE
Risk more/gain more   1–2–3–4–5 Protect what have/minimize
(confidence)   mistakes
LEARNING
Open/shared/value diversity   1–2–3–4–5 Directed/individual/single-minded

Attitude—How win

STRATEGY
Premium price/service/innovation   1–2–3–4–5 Low cost/low-service/min. viable
FOCUS
Divergence from competitors   1–2–3–4–5 Convergence on market leader
POSTURE
Proactive/breakthrough   1–2–3–4–5 Responsive/reliable
innovation   steady progress

(continued)

TOOL 1.1   BRAVE Culture Assessment/Preference (continued)

Relationships—How Connect

POWER, DECISION-MAKING
Diffused/debated—confront issues   1–2–3–4–5 Controlled/monarchical
DIVERSITY, EQUITY, INCLUSION
All welcome, valued, respected   1–2–3–4–5 Bias to work with people
                                              just like us
COMMUNICATION, CONTROLS
Informal/verbal/face-to-face   1–2–3–4–5 Formal/directed/written

Behaviors—What Impact

WORKING UNITS
One org. Interdependent teams   1–2–3–4–5 Independent individuals, units
DISCIPLINE
Fluid/flexible (guidelines)   1–2–3–4–5 Structured/disciplined (polices)
DELEGATION
Inspire, enable, empower, trust   1–2–3–4–5 Narrow task-focused direction

TOOL 1.2

6 Cs Situation Analysis

Consider the following items as a framework for gathering information and drawing conclusions both opportunistically and proactively during your onboarding period. See Tool 1.3 and pull it all together in a SWOT analysis (Strengths, Weaknesses, Opportunities, and Threats) to help draw conclusions about:

- Sources, drivers, hinderers of revenue, and value
- Current strategy/resource deployment: Coherent? Adequate?
- Insights and scenarios

1. **Customers** (First line, customer chain, end users, influencers)

    Needs, hopes, preference, commitment, strategies, price/value perspective by segment:

First Line/Direct Customers

- Universe of opportunity—total market, volume by segment
- Current situation—volume by customer; profit by customer

Customer Chain

- Customers' customers—total market, volume by segment
- Current customers' strategies, volume, and profitability by segment

End Users

- Preference, consumption, usage, loyalty, and price value data and perceptions for our products and competitors' products

Influencers

- Key influencers of customer and end user purchase and usage decisions

2. **Collaborators** (Suppliers, business allies, partners, government/ community leaders)

- Strategies, profit/value models for external and internal stakeholders (up, across, down)

3. **Culture**

- Behaviors—What impact (implementation)
- Relationships—How connect (communication)
- Attitudes—How to win (choices)
- Values—What matters and why (purpose)
- Environment—Where to plan (context)

4. **Capabilities**

- Human (includes style and quality of management, strategy dissemination, culture, values, norms, focus, discipline, innovation, teamwork, execution, urgency, politics)
- Operational (includes integrity of business processes, effectiveness of organization structure, links between measures and rewards, and corporate governance)
- Financial (includes capital and asset utilization and investor management)

(continued)

TOOL 1.2   6 Cs Situation Analysis (continued)

- Technical (includes core processes, IT systems, and supporting skills)
- Key assets (includes brands and intellectual property)

5. **Competitors** (Direct, indirect, potential)
   - Strategies, profit/value models, profit pools by segment, source of pride

6. **Conditions**
   - Social/demographic—trends
   - Political/government/regulatory—trends
   - Economic—macro and micro—trends
   - Market definition, inflows, outflows, substitutes—trends
   - Macro health and climate change impact on your organization

TOOL 1.3
SWOT

Internal   External

Internal		External
Strengths	Key Leverage Points	Opportunities
Weaknesses	Business Issues	Threats
	Sustainable Competitive Advantage	

Strengths	Internal to organization—things we do better
Weaknesses	Internal to organization—things we do worse
Opportunities	External to organization—things to capitalize on
Threats	External to organization—things to worry about

Key Leverage Points

Opportunities we can leverage our strengths against (where play to win)

Business Implications

Threats our weaknesses make us vulnerable to (where play not to lose)

Sustainable Competitive Advantages

Key leverage points that can be sustained over extended period of time

---

TOOL 1.4

Risk Assessment

For each of the components below, estimate the level of risk for each land mine on a scale of 1–4: 1 = low; 2 = manageable; 3 = mission-crippling; 4 = insurmountable. Then look at the individual rankings to come up with an overall risk assessment.

Organization: Assess risks of organization's strategy and ability to implement (1–2–3–4):

(Look for the organization's sustainable competitive advantage)

Role: Assess risks of stakeholders' alignment around expectations and resources (1–2–3–4):

(Understand who had concerns about the role and what was done to address them)

Personal: Assess risk of gaps in your strengths, motivation, or fit (1–2–3–4):

(Understand what, specifically, about you led to your getting the offer)

Relationships: Assess risks in your ability to build and maintain key relationships (1–2–3–4):

(*continued*)

TOOL 1.4   Risk Assessment (continued)

Learning: Assess risks in your ability to gain adequate information and knowledge (1–2–3–4)

Delivery: Assess risks in your ability to build a high-performing team that can deliver fast enough (1–2–3–4)

Adjustment: Assess risks in your ability to see or react to situational changes down the road (1–2–3–4)

Assess overall risk and if it's

> **Relatively low**, do nothing out of the ordinary (but keep your eyes open for the inevitable changes).
>
> **Manageable**, manage it in the normal course of your job.
>
> **Mission-crippling**, resolve before accepting the job or mitigate before doing anything else.
>
> **Insurmountable**, walk away.

CHAPTER 2

The Job Starts When You Accept the Offer

LEVERAGE THE FUZZY FRONT END.

Converge				Pivot		Evolve			
Day One				30	45	60	70	100	
Position Yourself for success	Leverage the Fuzzy Front End	Take control of Day One	Lay your Leadership Foundation	Co-create Burning Imperative	Embed Milestone Management	Invest in Early Wins	Realign Team	Adjust and Advance	

WARNING!

If you have already started your new role, this chapter may upset you. It is full of ideas for people to implement before they start. The best way to take charge, build your team, and deliver better results faster than anyone thought possible is to create time by starting earlier than anyone thought you would.

Like it or not, a new leader's role begins as soon as that person is an acknowledged candidate for the job and certainly begins at the moment they accept. Everything new leaders do and say and don't do and don't say will send powerful signals, starting well before they even walk in the door on Day One.

This fuzzy front end between accepting and starting is a golden opportunity. Those taking advantage of that time do dramatically better in the early days of their new role. Those not taking advantage of that time tend to have much less pleasant experiences. The prescription is relatively simple. Take advantage of the time. Plan. Get set up. Invest in relationships, learning, and messaging. Listen.

Choose the Right Day to Be Day One

One subtle way of creating time is to take control of the start date. If there's flexibility—which is not always the case—you might negotiate a start date that allows a longer fuzzy front end and therefore more time for helpful activities before Day One. Alternatively, you might separate your actual first day on the payroll from the publicly announced first day. By having a private Day One that your boss knows about and a later public Day One, you can accomplish things while you are an employee, but before you start getting pulled into the normal day-to-day routine, thereby stretching your fuzzy front end.

The Longer the Better

At first, Nathaniel did not buy the concept that he should start before his official Day One. He wanted to take some time off so that he could show up at his new job rested and relaxed. Further, he felt uncomfortable asking for meetings before he was officially on the job. Eventually, he agreed to try several of our suggested actions before Day One.

Here is exactly what he wrote to us in an e-mail one week later:

"I've already reached out to some future colleagues and some agency counterparts just to introduce myself. You're right, it is game changing. Everyone has reacted with warmth and candor, and it will make the first few weeks far more productive, effective, and enjoyable."

As laid out next and in Tool 2.1, the personal 100-Day Worksheet, make your fuzzy front end even more powerful with these six steps:

1. Determine your leadership approach given the context and culture you face.
2. Identify key stakeholders.
3. Craft your entry message using your current best thinking.
4. Jump-start key relationships and accelerate your learning.
5. Manage your personal and office setup.
6. Plan your Day One, early days, and first 100 days.

1. Determine Your Leadership Approach Given the Context and Culture You Face

Step one is to identify the organization's need for change and its readiness for change. The context (the circumstances that create the setting) you're facing determines how fast you *should* move (need for change). The current culture determines how fast and effectively you *can* move (readiness for change).

Start by Analyzing the Context

When determining the need for change, the key question is: How significantly and how fast does the organization need to change to achieve its mission and goals, given its business environment, history, and recent performance?

1. **Business Environment:** You already assessed the business environment with your 6 Cs analyses during due diligence. Be sure to look for trends within each C: customers, collaborators, culture, capabilities, competitors, and conditions.

2. **Organization History:** Understanding how the organization got to its current state can give you invaluable insight into the drivers for change as well as the roots of individual team members' assumptions about the situation. Go back as far as you can to understand things such as the founder's intent, heroes along the way, and the stories and myths that people carry around with them.

3. **Recent Business Performance:** Dig below the obvious in looking at recent business performance. Understand the components of the overall numbers to get at what is working well and less well. Identify absolute and relative results, recent trends, positive and negative drivers, and whether they are temporary blips or enduring obstacles. Use Tool 2.2 to help with your context assessment.

4. **Role Expectations:** Now compare the expectations, objectives, and changes in ambition that have been explained to you (for your role and team) by those you met during interviews and

due diligence against your analysis of the business environment, the organization's history, and the recent business performance to determine how well (or poorly) positioned the organization is to achieve those expectations and objectives. Are those ambitions out of whack with the current business environment, the way the company has historically operated, or recent business performance? This will give you a sense of how fast things need to change and how pronounced a point of inflection you're facing.

Look at Overall Culture and Specific Individuals to Assess the Readiness for Change

Now that you have determined the organization's need for change, it is time to assess the organization's cultural readiness to accept, embrace, lead, and adapt to change. Readiness to change requires a combination of self-awareness, will, skill, and capacity. Members of the organization must understand the need for change, have the desire to change, have the know-how to change, and have the bandwidth to take on the additional work associated with change.

Your first look at this will be derived from the cultural assessment you did during your due diligence (or should do now). When working with merging or newly reorganized teams, remember to assess the readiness for change for the combined or new organization, starting with the new leadership team.

HOT TIP

Look well beyond the professed culture: It's not that people lie about their preferences. It's just that value statements and creeds are often aspirational. You must understand the norms of behaviors, relationships, attitudes, values, and the work environment that people default to "when the boss is not around." That is almost always a more accurate indication of the true culture of the organization rather than the culture defining statements you may find emblazoned on the company website.

Determine Your Leadership Approach

At this point, you've assessed whether cultural change is needed and whether the team is ready. Now you are ready to choose how to best engage with the existing culture by assimilating, converging and evolving, or shocking the organization (ACES).

After the decision to take the job in the first place, this may be the most important decision you make ahead of your first 100 days. It is difficult, if not impossible, to recover from a wrong cultural engagement choice. Your choice is dependent upon the environment you're walking into and the existing culture's readiness for change. Tool 2.3 will help you determine the most appropriate approach for your situation as illustrated in Figure 2.1.

It is a critical choice, but if you do the analysis properly the following guidelines should steer you toward the correct approach:

> **Assimilate** when your analysis indicates that urgent change is not required to deliver the expected results and the readiness for change exists as reflected in a cohesive team in place. You can figure out the minor changes you need to make over time together with your team and your stakeholders. This is a wonderful but rare situation.

FIGURE 2.1   Context and Culture Decision Tool

Context	Ready to Accelerate	Facing Disaster
Strong need to change	**Converge and Evolve Quickly**	**Shock**
	Smooth Sailing	Unstable Calm
Less need to change right now	**Assimilate**	**Converge and Evolve Slowly**

Culture

Ready to change	Not ready to change

In most cases, you'll want to converge and evolve. If this is your approach, you'll also want to be mindful of the speed in which you do so.

Converge and Evolve Slowly when your analysis indicates that *urgent change is not required* but slight adjustments will be needed over time to fully deliver the expected results, yet the *culture is not ready to change* to support the required adjustments. If this is your chosen approach, you will first become part of the organization, and then slowly start to implement the changes that are required. Often, a way to start this change is with a series of carefully thought through small step changes, deployed over time.

Converge and Evolve Quickly when your analysis indicates that significant changes are required immediately to deliver expected results and the *culture is ready* for change. You may be the catalyst that helps the organization wake up to the urgent need for change. *Quickly* is the word—too slow and failure will catch you.

Shock when *significant changes must be made immediately* to deliver the expected results and when the culture is *not ready* to change. In this scenario, you have a truly challenging situation. You must shock the system for it to survive. You must do it immediately. And the going will be tough. Know that this is extraordinarily risky and that you may end up as a dead hero, paving the way for your successor to complete a transformation you couldn't survive yourself. Be advised that this is rarely the appropriate choice.

Identify What You Need to Do Differently as a Leader in This Specific Situation

Once you've assessed the situation and determined your leadership approach, think hard about what you need to do differently, behaviorally, to lead the team. What will you need to dial up, or dial down, in terms of overall leadership style in your new role versus how you've led in the past? What behaviors will you need to emphasize more in this new role? And as a result, how will you need to change the way you allocate your time between "Doing" and "Managing/Leading" across the different functions or initiatives you're accountable for per Tool 2.4 at the end of the chapter?

Mergers, Reorganizations, Turnarounds, and Transformations Require Special Attention

When leading teams that are about to be merged or reorganized, *converge and evolve* is almost always the best approach. Pure *assimilation* will be too slow, and the benefits of synergies may never be realized. If you deploy a *shock* approach, you will miss the opportunity to clarify roles and enroll new players in the definition of future state. Remember—people will not pay attention to anything to do with strategy or execution of a new, combined vision (no matter how obvious or exciting to senior management) until they are confident in *their own role* and who *their colleagues and collaborators* will be in the new organization.

In a turnaround or transformation, be prepared to lead with an approach of Shock or Converge and Evolve Quickly, as the need for change is high, creating a more urgent need to get the team's attention and define a new path to success.

It is critical to get this right. Think this through early, use your best preliminary assessment to decide your leadership approach, test your hypothesis during your fuzzy front end, and then reassess your choice just before Day One. Finally, especially in the early days and weeks, urge your boss and other trusted key stakeholders to slow you down or speed you up as you gain a stronger feel for the culture's ability to accept and adapt to change.

2. Identify Key Stakeholders

Step two of the fuzzy front end is to identify your key stakeholders. These are the people who can have the most impact on your success in your new role. Many transitioning executives fail to think this through completely or look in only one direction to find their key stakeholders. Others make the mistake of treating everyone the same and end up trying to please all of them. To avoid these mistakes, look in all directions to find your key stakeholders:

> *Up* stakeholders may include your boss, your indirect boss if there is a matrix organization, your boss's boss, the board of directors,

your boss's assistant, or anyone else who resides further up in the organization.

Across stakeholders might include key allies, peers, partners, and even the person who wanted your job but didn't get it. The across stakeholders that executives often forget are key clients, customers, suppliers, and partners. Look internal and external to the organization.

Down stakeholders usually include your direct reports, their direct reports, and other critical people who are essential to successful implementation of your team's goals. Your executive assistants should be high on this list, because they can often serve as additional sets of eyes and ears.

Former stakeholders: If you're getting promoted from within or making a lateral move, make sure to take into account your up, across, and down stakeholders from your former position. Some of them may still be impactful to success or failure in your new role.

Internal board: Your internal board is made up of the people you are going to treat differently because of their influence or impact regardless of their explicit roles in the hierarchy. You're going to treat them like board members, never surprising them in meetings and making sure that they get the chance to give you informal, off-the-record advice. Set the stage early and position yourself as an executive who is eager for and welcomes feedback from your internal board.

Some key stakeholders will be apparent, yet others are often hidden from view, so do not be afraid to ask your human resources contact, boss, predecessor, buddy, or mentor when you are building your list. Throughout, have a bias to keep more people on the list rather than less—at least to start. Ignoring a key stakeholder can have a devastating impact on a new leader and might kill any chance of a successful transition.

Similarly, have a bias to treat people with more respect rather than less. If you are unsure where stakeholders fit on your list, it's always better to upgrade a stakeholder. You are not going to get in much trouble treating an *across* like an *up* or a *down* like an *across*. The opposite is not true. And be explicit about diversity, equity, and inclusion opportunities and risks to make sure you're treating everyone with the respect they deserve.

Identify Those Committed, Contributing, Watching, and Detracting

Inevitably, some of your stakeholders will support what you're trying to do, some will resist it, and some will sit on the sidelines and watch for a while. Call them committed, contributing, watching, and detracting, respectively.

> **Committed:** The committed are driven by the purpose, the cause, and doing good for others. They believe and will do whatever it takes to accomplish the desired results. Keep them committed with simple direct communication that touches their emotions and gets them to believe viscerally in what you're trying to do together.
>
> **Contributors:** These are the people who share your vision and have been working for change. Often, they are new to the company or role, so they see that there's more to gain by going forward with the new leader's plan than by holding on to the past. Enroll these people as allies.
>
> **Watchers:** The compliant are primarily driven by what is good for them and concerned about their basic needs. Compliant people aren't hurting the organization, but they are not primary drivers of change. They are doing what they are told and no more. These are your watchers and will probably stay watchers. The goal is to make them aware of what they need to do and make sure it gets done.
>
> **Detractors:** These are the people who are comfortable with the status quo, fear looking incompetent, perceive a threat to their values/power, fear negative consequences for their key allies, and may have been in the position for a long time, so they have more to lose in giving up the current state than they have to gain by supporting a perceived risky change.

Some have disengaged and checked out emotionally. They don't believe in the platform for change, the vision, or the call to action. They won't do what the organization needs them to do. Their complete disconnect qualifies them as detractors. If they don't immediately respond to the new messaging, move them out, quickly.

Note that people with high levels of current power have a bias to resist change because they have more to lose than to gain, as illustrated

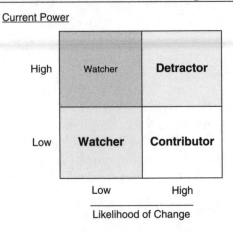

FIGURE 2.2   Power and Change

in Figure 2.2. It's not always the case, but it is true in enough situations for you to be particularly thoughtful in developing relationships with these people.

As a leader, you have only so much energy to expend on influencing your team. The overall prescription is to move every influencer one step in the right direction. In general, keep the committed in the loop and then start by increasing the commitment level of your contributors. Then move the convincible watchers into contributors. Don't try to turn detractors into contributors in one fell swoop. Try and move them from detractors to watchers and then possibly to contributors over time. Get those that remain detractors out of the way.

Finally, a word about *onboarding buddies*. As you work through your fuzzy front end and early days, be alert to the opportunity to request additional support from a peer or other experienced, influential member of the team.

Answer each one of the following questions with your entire target audience in mind:

- What are they currently thinking and doing? What's most important to them?
- What do they need to stop doing, keep doing, or change how they are doing it?
- What do they need to know to move them from their current state to the desired state?

Dig Deep to Identify Critical Stakeholders During Mergers and Turnarounds

When leading a post-merger integration, take extra time with the acquired company's leadership team to understand who the key players and influencers are, as they do not always match with the most senior titles.

Similarly, the agents of change and influence who are so critical to the success of a turnaround are often found on the front lines, working with customers, partners, and field team members to design and implement improvements and innovations. Look past the board room and leadership team to find those hidden champions.

3. Craft Your Entry Message Using Your Best Current Thinking

Step three of the fuzzy front end is to craft your entry message.

Before you start talking to any of your stakeholders, think through with whom you are communicating. Be as specific as you can and include everyone and all groups that can have an impact, including your target, their primary influencers, and other influencers.

Next, you'll want to clarify your initial message.

Crafting and deploying your message has to do with the words you use (and don't) and the actions you take (and don't). Be conscious of your choices and craft an intentional entry message before you start talking to stakeholders. You are going to get positioned in people's minds either by what others tell them about you or by what you say and do. You're always better off taking control of as much of that as you can. This requires an entry message about the change you will bring, which you should evolve as you learn.

Start by putting a stake in the ground with your current best thinking to craft your entry message. Use that to help with your directed learning and evolve as you learn.

As you start your new role, recall that inertia is a powerful force and you can't get people to do anything different unless they believe they cannot keep doing what they were doing before (that is your platform for change), they can picture themselves in a better place (that's the vision), and they know their part in solving the problem (their call to action). Your headline and communication points flow from the platform for change, the vision, and the call to action.

1. **Platform for change (Why):** These are the facts, stimuli, and revelations that will make your audience realize they need to do something different from what they have been doing. (Note people react better to an external platform for change outside their control than to being told that something they are doing is not good enough.)

2. **Vision (What):** This is the picture of a brighter future that your audience can picture themselves in. Not your vision. Theirs.

3. **Call to action (How):** These are specific actions the audience can take to get there so they can be part of the solution.

Once you have thought through these foundational points, consider how you need to be viewed as a leader in this situation, and distill all of that down to one driving message (your headline or bumper sticker) and your main communication points. Remember that your audience is always asking, "What does this mean for me?" Use the "Message" section in Tool 2.1 to capture this information and Tool 2.5 to help plan your communication.

HOT TIP

Get your message vaguely right immediately. Of course, you're not going to go preach your message on or before Day One. You're going to evolve it over time. But you can't avoid inadvertently sending the wrong message until you know the right message for you, for them, for the vision, and for the moment.

4. Jump-Start Key Relationships and Accelerate Your Learning Before Day One

Step four of the fuzzy front end is to jump-start key relationships and accelerate your learning. These two items work hand-in-hand. You achieve this by conducting prestart meetings and phone calls *now*, before you start. The impact you can make by reaching out to critical stakeholders before you start is incalculable. Yet some executives are surprisingly reluctant to set up those meetings. They often expect to encounter resistance but rarely do.

First, using your list of key stakeholders, determine which ones you should meet with, video, or speak with before Day One. The most important stakeholders are the ones who are going to be most critical to your surviving and thriving in the new role.

These might include:

- Your new boss
- The most influential board members
- Critical peers—especially ones who were candidates for your new job
- Critical customers and clients
- Critical direct reports—especially high performers, those with critical skill sets, ones who were candidates for your new job, or those who are valuable and considered flight risks

Leverage the Fuzzy Front End to Get Real Answers and Perspective

Another reason to start communicating with key stakeholders early is that the answers you get to questions before you start will be different from the answers you get after you start. You are a different person before you start. You are not yet an employee or boss. You are just someone looking to make a connection and learn. The answers you get during the fuzzy front end almost always prove exceedingly valuable after Day One.

There are times when fuzzy front end meetings or even video meetings may not be possible, or a potential stakeholder may be unwilling. Even so, just asking for the premeeting makes a favorable impact.

HOT TIP

Meet with critical stakeholders before you start—or at least video with them one-on-one. This one idea is worth a gazillion times whatever you paid for this book. Contacting key stakeholders before you start always makes a huge difference. It is a game changer.

Now that you have your prestart conversations set, it is important to have an approach for those conversations. These conversations are most successful when you are talking as little as possible and listening as attentively as possible. They are about building relationships and learning.

In a wonderful TED Talk on "The Power of Vulnerability," researcher/storyteller Brené Brown explained that making a connection with someone else requires us to let them really see us, leaving ourselves vulnerable to harm.[1] These early prestart conversations are your first best chance to let your guard down, be vulnerable, and make connections with your most important stakeholders by asking for their help in terms of their read on the situation, priorities, and "how things are done around here."

Because this is about relationships first, your first question will probably be something along the lines of "Tell me about yourself." You want to connect with your key stakeholders individually. You want to understand their personal wants and needs as well as their business issues. This may also be a good time to take your crafted message out for a test drive; but keep in mind this is not about you, so keep your message short and on point. Because you are here to build relationships and learn, it is not the time to tell your life story or to offer opinions on how things should be done.

Structuring the conversations is useful. Come into these conversations with an open mind, and actively listen to what your key stakeholders have to say. Doing so in a planned and thoughtful way is fundamental to maximizing the value of these conversations. Break the conversations into learning, expectations, and implementation. Tool 2.6 will help.

Strengths and Perceptions

After learning a little about them personally, probe people's read on the general situation. Focus on two key areas: strengths and perceptions. Ask people what strengths and capabilities are required for success versus their perceptions of what is in place now. Notice the differences. This is not a search for the one truth. This is an exercise

---

[1] Brené Brown, 2010, "The Power of Vulnerability," TED Talk video, 20:19, June.

in understanding the different stakeholders' perceptions so you can better lead and communicate with them once you take charge.

When you receive answers to your questions, ask for examples that might reinforce the answers. We all communicate with stories. Beginning in the fuzzy front end, drop any reference to your former organization, and immediately switch the *we* in your conversations to make it clear that you consider yourself part of the new organization. If you manage these conversations well, you should have several new *we* stories to use as examples going forward.

Expectations

The objectives of the conversations with your stakeholders will be different up, across, and down. Therefore, your questions will also be different for each group. Your *up* stakeholders' expectations around priorities and resources are direction for you. Your *across* stakeholders' expectations are input to build mutual understanding. Your *down* stakeholders' expectations are data to help you learn about their current reality and their needs.

This is also an excellent time to figure out if there are any *untouchables*. Untouchables are those things that may seem odd or do not have a natural fit with the larger goals of an organization or division but might be pet projects or protected people that you should not touch. Most organizations have them; and they can be the third rail for executives who don't recognize them as untouchables. Identify them early and let them be . . . at least at first.

Implementation

At this part of the conversation, you're looking to understand (1) control points (what things are measured, tracked, and reported and how), (2) how decisions are made, and (3) the best way to communicate with people.

Different organizations use different metrics and processes for controlling what is really going on. You'll need to understand what things are measured, tracked, and reported and how—and what is not being formally tracked but informally watched in the shadows.

Decision Rights

Understanding how decisions are made is about understanding who makes what decisions with whose input. There are five ways that you and another person can make decisions:

Level 1: I decide on my own.

Level 2: I decide with input from you.

Level 3: You and I decide together.

Level 4: You decide with my input.

Level 5: You decide on your own.

In general, you want to push decisions to Levels 2 and 4 (either you or your key stakeholder makes decisions with input from the other). Input is helpful whether it is veto rights, consultation, or information.

Shared decisions have a nasty tendency not to be made by anyone. Avoid putting yourself in that scenario.

That's the easy part. The trickier part is understanding where the real decision power resides. The three key sources of power are:

Deciders (Who makes the decisions? Who sets the rules?)

Influencers (Who holds opinions that matter, has sway or control?)

Implementers (Who controls the resources required to implement decisions?)

It is important to consider how they interact and how they impact the organization when you are establishing your decision-making process. Each of your key stakeholders could play any of those roles or none of them at any given time. It's important to figure out when your key stakeholders can leverage those sources of power.

Communication Preferences

Use these fuzzy front end prestart meetings to begin to understand stakeholders' communication preferences. Pay particular attention to mode, manner, frequency, and disagreements.

- **Mode** refers to the type of communication: e-mail, text, voicemail, in person, and so on.

- **Manner** is the style of communication: more formal and disciplined or less. Note especially if they prefer to have something to read and digest prior to your conversations.

- **Frequency** is how often people prefer to be communicated with: daily updates, weekly, only when the project is completed, and so on.

- **Disagreements.** Different people prefer being disagreed with in different ways, ranging from:

  1. Never disagree with me.

  2. Challenge me one-on-one, but only in private.

  3. Challenge me in team meetings, but never let anyone outside "the family" know what you're thinking.

  4. Challenge me in any meetings, but gently.

  5. Gloves off, all the time, because public challenges communicate the culture we want.

Ask about this, but don't believe the initial answers you get. Initially, start at the top of the list, and wait to see how your key stakeholders, and especially your boss, respond to disagreements and challenges from others before you start disagreeing with them or challenging them.

Don't Trust Your Instincts

As an executive onboarding into a new role, *do not trust your first impressions and instincts.*[2] You don't understand your new situation, team, and organization as well as you knew your old ones. That means that thinking and acting in your new job the way you did before in your previous organization is fraught with danger.

Daniel Kahneman, notable for his work on the psychology of judgement and decision-making, describes this as intuitive thinking.

---

[2] George Bradt, 2017, "Follow This Nobel Prize Winner's Advice as an Executive Onboarding into a New Role," *Forbes*, August 9.

In his 2002 Nobel Prize lecture, he described intuition as "thoughts and preferences that come to mind quickly and without much reflection" as opposed to a more deliberate, controlled, effortful, rule-governed way of thinking through things. Our intuitions are often wrong if we don't consider biases like accessibility, framing, and attribution.

Follow Kahneman's advice, and ours, and be sure to apply more deliberate thinking in the fuzzy front end.

Competence

The insights of Kahneman and his partner Amos Tversky go hand-in-hand with the conscious competence model. As people learn new skills, they go from unconsciously incompetent (don't know what they don't know) to consciously incompetent (know what they don't know and aren't happy about it) to consciously competent (can do with deliberative thinking) to unconsciously competent (can do intuitively).

When you move into a new organization or a meaningfully different new role, you go from being competent to incompetent. If you're unconsciously incompetent you're going to get into trouble because you'll be relying on your old intuitions. If you're consciously incompetent, you can ratchet yourself up to conscious competence with deliberative thinking. (It's the difference between driving off the ferry from the United Kingdom to France and not knowing, versus knowing you're supposed to drive on the right side of the road in France.)

5. Manage Your Personal and Office Setup

Step five of the fuzzy front end is to manage your personal and office setup well before Day One. No matter how much you try, you cannot give the new job your best efforts until you get comfortable about your family's setup. Taking the time to figure out housing, schools, transportation, and the like is not a luxury. It is a business imperative. The more drastic the move, the more issues you'll need to solve.

Similarly, make sure someone is getting your office set up before Day One. This doesn't have to be done perfectly because you can evolve as you go, though do make sure your office sends the right message about your approach: formal versus informal, functional versus welcoming.

There is no better time to get these resolved than during the fuzzy front end. If you wait, these things will distract you at a time when everyone is making those first and lasting impressions of your performance. Leverage the checklists at the end of this chapter to help get these done well before Day One.

Finally, make sure your human resources partner is accommodating your needs and helping you assimilate culturally and accelerate your plan, so you can ensure an impactful Day One. Tools 2.7 and 2.8 will help.

6. Plan Your Day One, Early Days, and First 100 Days

Step six of the fuzzy front end is to plan your Day One, early days, and first 100 days. There is a lot to learn in the fuzzy front end. The tools presented in this chapter will guide you along the way, but they are not designed to be all-inclusive. Instead, think of this process as a starting point for your entry into your new role. If you follow the process to this point, you will have completed a reasonably in-depth dive into your new organization's people, plans, practices, and purpose.

The knowledge gathered from your due diligence and your own self-study, coupled with what you learn in your prestart conversations, should enable you to begin to put things in context and help you figure out what you want to do on that first day, during that first week, and during those first 100 days. With this knowledge base, you can use Tool 2.1 at the end of this chapter to begin the outline of your 100-Day Plan. One of the most important choices you must make is how to engage the culture (Shock, Assimilate, or Converge and Evolve). So reconfirm that choice at the end of your fuzzy front end, just before you head into Day One.

The fuzzy front end approach detailed here will be effective in almost any scenario, no matter the role, function, or industry. Follow it and you'll be well on your way to better results faster. Some situations are unique enough to warrant slight enhancements or additional steps. Five circumstances where you might want to manage your fuzzy front end differently:

- Onboarding remotely
- Getting promoted from within

- Leading a merger/acquisition
- Leading a turnaround or restart
- Making an international move

There's more on leading a merger/acquisition and leading a turnaround or restart in separate chapters later and more on each of these at primegenesis.com/tools.

Manage Remote Onboarding Differently

For a variety of reasons, the global workforce is becoming increasingly remote from the physical office. Certain crises have exacerbated the trend and it's expected to continue in this direction. Employees demand it. And technology enables it. As such, it's a very real possibility that you could be beginning your new job remotely without ever having met your key stakeholders in person.

Executives onboarding into new roles have to communicate and connect at a feeling and attitudinal level to establish trusting relationships. This is best done face-to-face in as small a group and intimate a setting as practical.

In cases where live, face-to-face meetings are not warranted or not allowed because of a crisis or some other reason, bridge as much of the "physical gap" as possible by using videoconferencing tools. Face-to-face communication is always valuable but even more so when there will be an undetermined time lag before you get the chance to meet stakeholders in person. Phone calls are the next best choice. Give people extra time and space to explain their feelings and attitudes when meeting them remotely.

Albert Mehrabian, a professor at UCLA's Department of Psychology, studied communication for decades. In his book *Silent Messages* he presents his findings about nonverbal communication and how people draw conclusions about feelings and attitudes about a person and their message.[3] He states:

- 7% of feelings and attitudes are derived from the words that are spoken.

---

[3] Albert Mehrbabian, 1971, *Silent Messages*, Mason, OH: Wadsworth Pub. Co.

- 38% of feelings and attitudes are derived from paralinguistics, or the way the words are said or tone of voice.

- 55% of feelings and attitudes are derived from facial expression.

Feelings and attitudes are strong considerations whether people like or dislike a message and the messenger. If you heed Professor Mehrabian's and our advice you'll get the best results if you heavily weight your remote onboarding experience to include as much face-to-face communications (videoconferencing tools) as possible.

Remote onboarding also calls for more frequent interactions, with a mix of "strictly business" and personal "get-to-know" conversations to compensate for the lack of "watercooler" opportunities. Mixing up small groups around information-sharing and problem-solving can also provide insights into culture during times you're forced to remain remote from the team.

Manage Getting Promoted from Within Differently

Although the basics of this chapter apply to both getting promoted from within and making a lateral transfer, there are some important differences:

You can't control the context—so prepare in advance; be ready to adjust as required. Understand the context (planned, unplanned, or interim). Secure the resources and support you need. Go with the flow, regain control of the situation, or jump into the dirty work as appropriate.

If it's interim, get clarity on whether that means "holding the fort until we find the right person, which absolutely will not be you," "on probation with a good chance of becoming permanent," or "doing the job as a developmental opportunity on the way to something else." In either case, engaging fully with the work itself while eschewing the perks of the job implies focusing your efforts on the least prestigious, highest impact tasks and leaving the glory to others.

It's hard to make a clean break. So take control of your own message and transition. Manage the announcement cascade (Tool 2.9). Secure your base, ensuring your *old* area's ongoing success and recognizing the people who helped you along the way. Then use part of the time before you start to assess your predecessor's legacy, what you'll keep and change.

There is no honeymoon, as others will assume you already know the organization, its priorities, and culture. So set or reinforce direction and generate momentum quickly after the start. Evolve the stated and de facto strategies and then improve operations and strengthen your organization at the right pace.

Summary and Implications

During the fuzzy front end, you should:

1. Determine your leadership approach given the context and culture you face.
2. Identify key stakeholders up, down, and across.
3. Craft your entry message using current best thinking.
4. Jump-start key relationships and accelerate your learning.
5. Manage your personal and office setup.
6. Plan your Day One, early days, and first 100 days.

Although this approach is generally applicable, there are some important differences in certain situations, such as onboarding remotely; getting promoted from within; managing a merger, acquisition, reorganization, or turnaround; or making an international move.

QUESTIONS YOU SHOULD ASK YOURSELF

What is the right leadership approach given the context and culture I face?

Who are my key stakeholders up, down, and across and whom do I need to engage for support during this process?

What is my entry message using current best thinking?

Note the most up-to-date, full, editable versions of all tools are downloadable at primegenesis.com/tools.

TOOL 2.1
Personal 100-Day Worksheet

Why did you want this job? Fill in initial thoughts on why you accepted, why the job/role is right for you.

What is the job? Fill in company, title, role, what you and your team are supposed to get done—goals and priorities, impact on others—within the context of the organization's objectives and strategies (as you understand them now). [1] How is this role different than your previous roles? What will you need to do differently as a leader in this role?

Why did they pick you? Fill in your understanding of what made you the right choice for the job/role. Which of your strengths do they most value and why do they think you will fit into their culture across behaviors, relationships, attitudes, values, and environment so you can do their job their way?

Leadership Approach based on an assessment of the Context, Culture and Risks

1. **Context**—How much change is needed in this organization, from less need to strong need?[2]
2. **Culture**—How ready is the organization to change, from not ready to ready to change?[3]
3. **Organization, role, and personal risk**—Is the risk low, manageable, mission-crippling, or insurmountable?[4]

Blend 1, 2, and 3 to determine Leadership approach: Assimilate | Converge & Evolve (Quickly or Slowly) | Shock **[Pick one]**

Communication

Stakeholders. Fill in names/titles of the few most critical stakeholders, noting diversity, equity, and inclusion (DE&I) opportunities and risks.

> **Up:** Your boss, their boss, board members (shadow board members), main shareholders, debt owners, and any other people that can tell you what to do:

> **Across:** Internal peers, external and internal customers, external and internal suppliers, allies, complementors, government, regulators, community, media, analysts, activists, bloggers, influencers:

(continued)

Down: Direct reports, perhaps some indirect reports:

Message. The platform for change, vision, and call to action are your raw data to inform your headline and communication points. Focus on ideas first, words later, taking into account DE&I.

> **Platform for change:** WHY must/can we change? Look to external situation or ambition changes and purpose.
>
> **Vision:** WHAT brighter future can we picture ourselves in? What will success look like?
>
> **Call to action:** HOW can we take specific actions to get there?
>
> **How do I want or need to be perceived as a leader in this role?**
>
> **Headline:** The overarching bumper sticker/organizing concept (1–5 words) The core idea underpinning how you influence how others feel in what you say and do. The idea is more important than the specific words.
>
> **Main communication points**: The three main points:

Before Day One
Personal setup: Things to get family set if moving, office needs like Internet, computer, phone, passwords

Jump-start learning: Information to gather and digest across

1. *Technical learning*—the company's products, customers, technologies, systems, and processes
2. *Cultural learning*—behavioral, relationship, attitudinal norms, values and environment, including DE&I
3. *Political learning*—how decisions are made, who has the power to make them, and whose support you will need => Shared reality/ unwritten rules

Announcement cascade: Fill in plan for who should find out about your joining when, keeping in mind that those emotionally impacted should find out one-on-one ahead of others and those directly impacted should find out in a small group so they can ask questions before the larger group indirectly impacted finds out in a mass communication.

Moving into a new organization

a. Meet live or via one-on-one video with the few most critical stakeholders. Note which to use:

b. Have phone calls with other important stakeholders. Note which to use:

      [Getting promoted from within, hitting a restart button, or merging teams] (If applicable; otherwise, skip)

a. Identify the go-forward leadership team:

b. Meet live or via video with the individuals on the team to reassure them:

c. Have an initial leadership team meeting live or via video to co-create the announcement cascade

      (Who hears what, when, how—in advance, during, and after announcement):

Day One/Early Days

Specific actions for day one and early days. Who to meet with? When? What forum? What signals to send/how to reinforce message?

Fill in your official Day One date—likely when you're on the new payroll:

Fill in your effective Day One date—when you're actually leading your new team:

Welcome session: Generally, a broad meet and greet with no speeches. (If not possible, send out a 1- to 2-minute video telling people how you feel about joining the organization and working with them.)

New leader's/owner's assimilation session: With the top 15–25 people in your organization (can be run live or virtually)

Message in action: An activity that communicates your message. Be. **Do**. Say. (Live or virtually)

Meet live/site visits: Moving through stakeholders (live or virtually)

Phone/video calls: Moving through stakeholders

(continued)

TOOL 2.1   Personal 100-Day Worksheet (continued)

Tactical Capacity Building Blocks

How you're going to create a high-performing team:

Strategic	*Burning imperative*: likely a workshop for leadership team to co-create and commit to a compelling imperative together (either live or virtually) leading to a business plan. Use consultative approach if you do not have confidence in your team. Fill in approach (workshop or consult, live or virtual) and target date (likely by Day 30):
Operational	*Milestones:* jump-starting your operational process— likely by Day 45 This is the heart of your business plan—what's getting done by whom, when. Fill in start date: *Early wins:* must jump-start in first 60 days to deliver by end of 6 months. Fill in start date:
Organizational	*Roles:* pick date to make decisions about your team (then implement over time)
Communication	Other critical communication steps including daily/weekly/monthly/quarterly/annual meeting flows to update milestones, business reviews, strategic, operating, organizational plans:
Change	Steps to move contributors to committed champions, watchers to contributors, get management detractors out of the way and then embed changes in culture over time:
Self	*Accelerator:* self-assessment + stakeholder feedback to course-correct and sustain momentum.

---

1. One critical piece is understanding the core focus of the organization.

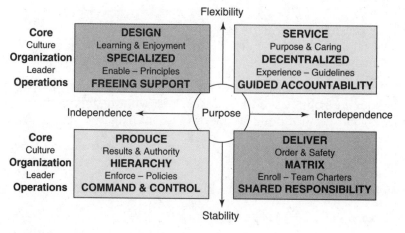

2. Assess the context by looking at:

    a. Historical context—from inception to this moment in time

    b. Recent results

    c. Business environment

        Also consider your 6 Cs analysis:

    Customers, Collaborators, Culture, Capabilities, Competitors, Conditions => SWOT

3. Asses the culture, and specific leaders, by considering:

    Awareness. Is the organization aware of the need for change [Low <=> High]?

    Will. Do they want to change [Low <=> High]?

    Skill. Do they have the know-how to change [Low <=> High]?

    Capacity. Do they have the bandwidth for change [Low <=> High]?

        Look at BRAVE dimensions: Behave, Relate, Attitude, Values, Environment, paying particular attention to evolving changes in sensibilities to work–life balance, health and well-being, relationships, our place in the world with regard to climate change and injustice (e.g., DE&I, religion, gender, LGBTQ)

4. If you want to go into greater depth on assessing your risk profile, you may want to consider

- Organization: From SWOT/sustainable competitive advantage
- Role: Mission and linkages with rest of the organization—sustain/evolve, start/restart
- Personal: Your strengths (innate talents, learned knowledge, practiced skills, hard-won experience, and, in rare cases, craft-level artistic caring and sensibilities), motivation (alignment with ideal job criteria and long-term goals), and fit between your preferred ways of working and the organizational culture

Context Assessment

Business Environment—6 Cs

Customers	Low satisfaction	......|......|......|......|......|......	Highly satisfied
Collaborators	Combative	......|......|......|......|......|......	Supportive
Culture	Unclear/ No impact	......|......|......|......|......|......	Clear/ Impactful
Capabilities	Lagging industry	......|......|......|......|......|......	Leading industry
Competitors	Ahead of us	......|......|......|......|......|......	Behind us
Conditions	Unfavorable	......|......|......|......|......|......	Favorable

Organizational History

Founder's intent:

Organizational heroes:

Guiding stories and myths:

Recent Business Performance

Absolute and relative results:

Recent Trends:

Positive drivers:

Negative drivers:

Need to change: Less urgent ......\|......\|......\|......\|......\|...... Urgent

TOOL 2.3

Context/Culture Map

Use this tool to map the organization's *need* and *readiness* to change and thus your approach.

	Converge & Evolve Quickly	Shock
Strong need to change		
No need to change right now	Assimilate	Converge & Evolve Slowly

                         Culturally ready to change   Culturally not ready to change

TOOL 2.4

Leadership Change

From	To
Previous Role	New Role

Leadership Style:

Behaviors:

Time Allocation:

Doing:

Item 1 (% of time)

Item 2 (% of time)

Item 3 (% of time)

Etc.

Managing/Leading:

Item 1 (% of time)

Item 2 (% of time)

Item 3 (% of time)

Etc.

TOOL 2.5
Communication Planning

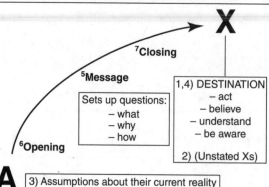

1. **Identify your destination.**

   What is the desired reaction and behavior you want from your audience/constituents?

   What specifically do you want, not want them to understand, believe, say about you, do?

2. **Be explicit about unstated Xs. What do you want the listener to think about you?**

3. **Assess current reality.**

   What does your audience/constituents currently understand, believe, say about you? Why?

   Develop a risk management plan including potential obstacles, negative rumors, sabotage, legal requirements, unintended consequences, and scenarios.

4. **Reevaluate destination in light of assumptions about audience.**

5. **Bridge the gap.**

   What do people need to be aware of, understand, and believe to move from current reality to your destination?

6. **Develop core messages and key communication points (maximum 5 core messages).**

7. **Package the message.**

   How should core messages be packaged for optimum effectiveness?

   What kind of supporting data do you need?

What is your key opening message?

What is your key closing message?

8. **Deliver the message.**

What are the best vehicles to reach your audience or constituents? What is optimum combination? What is the best timing to release the message? Who and what influences whom?

How do you best plant the follow-up seeds?

9. **Evolve.**

How should you modify your message based on what you've learned from your conversations and interactions with others?

TOOL 2.6

Onboarding Conversation Framework

Questions to ask during onboarding conversations (in addition to all the questions you would normally ask). Seek multiple perspectives, not necessarily one single truth.

1. **Learning**

What is your read on the general situation?

What strengths/capabilities are required?

Which strengths/capabilities exist now? Examples?

2. **Expectations**

What do you see as key priorities? Lower priorities? Current untouchables?

What resources are available to invest against these priorities?

3. **Implementation**

Tell me about the control points (metrics and process: meetings, reports).

Tell me about some of the key decisions we make. Who makes them? How?

What decision 1 A on own 2 A with B's input 3 Shared 4 B with A's input 5 B on own

What is the best way to communicate with you? (Mode/manner/frequency/disagreements?)

TOOL 2.7

Personal Setup Relocation Checklist

ASAP

Get set up: create move file, post calendar, and so on.

Choose a moving company. Get multiple bids and references.

Research schools at destination. Public? Independent?

Start to gather children's essential records in a secure folder that travels with you.

Choose a real estate agent at destination.

Make arrangements to sell or rent your current home.

Secure travel documents (passports, visas) and make travel arrangements for family and pets.

Research temporary housing options in case they become necessary.

Look hard at your possessions for things to give away or sell.

Start a log of moving expenses for employer or taxes.

Start to gather information about resources in destination city.

One Month Before Moving Day

Fill out change of address forms (for, e.g., IRS, subscriptions and bills).

Obtain medical and dental records, X-rays, and prescription histories.

Set up a checking account and safe deposit box in your new city/country.

Take inventory of your belongings before they are packed, ideally with pictures.

Arrange for help on moving day, especially looking after children.

Two Weeks Before Moving Day

Confirm travel reservations.

Clean rugs and clothing and have them wrapped for moving.

Close bank accounts and have your funds wired to your new bank.

Check with your insurance agent to ensure coverage through your homeowner's or renter's policy during the move.

Give a close friend or relative your travel route and schedule.

One Week Before Moving Day

Switch utility services to new address.

Prearrange for important services—such as a working phone.

Collect valuables (important documents, jewelry, etc.) from safe-deposit boxes, and so on.

On Move-Out Day

Be sure valuables are secure and ready to go with you. Carry important documents, currency, and jewelry yourself, or use registered mail.

If customary, have cash on hand to tip movers.

Have water, drinks, and snacks available for movers in appropriate place.

On Move-In Day

Have phone/camera on hand to record damages.

Have people ready to (1) check in items, (2) direct items to right place.

Have water, drinks, and snacks available for movers in appropriate place.

TOOL 2.8
Office Setup Checklist

Office (whose) or place to work

Desk

Chair

Office attitude (imposing and formal vs. welcoming and informal)

Visitor chairs

Couches

Tables

Cabinets

Whiteboards

Flip charts

Audiovisual

Employee #

Security Pass

Keys

Parking

Personal computer

Laptop

E-mail/system access

Phones/voicemail access

Cell phones

Stationery

Files

Business cards

Travel profile

Support

Executive Assistant

TOOL 2.9
Announcement Cascade

1. **Stakeholders** (internal and external)

   Emotionally impacted:

   Directly impacted:

   Indirectly impacted:

   Less impacted:

2. **Message**

   Platform for change: Headline:

   Vision: Message Points:

   Call to action:

---

3. **Pre-announcement Timeline** (one-on-ones, small groups, large groups)

   Prior to announcement day

   One-on-one:

   Announcement day

   One-on-one:

   Small groups:

4. **Formal Announcement**

   Method: Timing:

---

5. **Post-announcement Timeline** (one-on-ones, small groups, large groups, mass)

   One-on-one:

   Small groups:

   Large groups:

CHAPTER 3

Take Control of Day One

MAKE A POWERFUL FIRST IMPRESSION.
CONFIRM YOUR ENTRY MESSAGE.

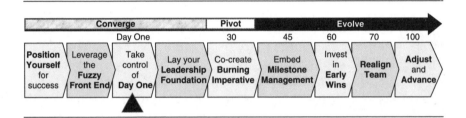

Our brains remember information "presented first and last and have an inclination to forget the middle items."[1] People will remember vividly their first impressions of you and their last interaction with you. Although you can update their last interaction constantly, you are going to be stuck with those first impressions. So be careful when choosing them. Be careful about the messages you send with your words, with your actions, with the order of your actions, and with the signs and symbols you deploy.

This is why Day One is such a meaningful pivot point for onboarding. Many people who are important to your new role will form their first, indelible impression of you on this day. As with the fuzzy front end, reconnect with your own behavior, relationship, attitude, value,

---

[1] Elizabeth Hilton, 2001, "Differences in Visual and Auditory Short-Term Memory," *Indiana University South Bend Journal*, 4.

and environment (BRAVE) preferences and approach, and think carefully about whom you are encountering and already starting to influence.

There is no one right way to manage your Day One, but there are many wrong ways to do it. It is all about the first impression received. Different people will have different impressions of the same thing depending on their perspective and filters. The problem is that before your first interactions with them, you can't understand their perspective and filters. So not only is there no one right answer, but it also can be difficult to figure out the best answer for your specific situation. Keep in mind that whatever you do will send signals to anyone who is watching you, so make your choices carefully.

This is another reason it is so valuable to get a jump-start on relationships and learning during the fuzzy front end. One of the powerful things about embracing the fuzzy front end is that it enables you to manage the initial impressions you make on those key people outside the noise of Day One. Managed well, it will also help you make better choices about your early days. A strong fuzzy front end, coupled with a well-thought-out Day One, will go a long way to minimize the risk of making a bad first impression.

What Are You Going to Do on Day One?

That question, more than any other, stumps our clients. Most leaders fail to think about and plan Day One as thoroughly as it deserves. In fact, even those leaders who do a phenomenal job throughout the fuzzy front end find themselves stumbling on their first day. For some reason, leaders are often lulled into complacency when deciding what to do on Day One. Often, they passively accept a schedule that someone else has planned out for them. Or they plan to do what seems to be the traditional Day One activities of meeting those people around their office or filling out the required forms, unpacking, and setting up their office.

Not you. You're going to take control of your own onboarding. What you say and do on Day One is going to inspire others. Not with cheesy motivational tactics but through meaningful words and actions that create excitement about the things to come. Do not underestimate Day One's importance. Plan it with great care and make sure it communicates your message, exactly as you want it, to the people you most need to reach.

No two leaders' first days will ever be the same because the combination of variables in every situation begs for different Day One plans. However, when planning your Day One, here are some general guidelines and principles to consider:

It is personal. As a leader, you impact people's lives. These people will try hard to figure out you and your potential impact as soon as they can. They may even rush to judgment. Keep that in mind at all times.

Order counts. Be deliberate about the order in which you meet with people and the timing of when you do what throughout Day One and your early days. The order in which you do things should and *will* communicate what's important to you in your new role. Make sure the sequence you choose communicates what you want and doesn't communicate what you don't want.

Messages matter. Have a message. Know what you are going to say and not say. Have a bias toward listening. Know that strong opinions, long-winded introductions, and efforts to prove yourself immediately are rarely, if ever, good Day One tactics. People will be looking to form opinions early. Keep that in mind while deciding when to listen, when to share, what to ask, whom to ask, and how you answer. When you speak, keep it brief, on point, and meaningful.

Location counts. Think about where you will show up for work on Day One. Do not just show up at your designated office by default. This is especially true as more people are working remotely.

Signs and symbols count. Be aware of all the ways you communicate, well beyond just words. Think BRAVE!

Timing counts. Day One does not have to match the first day you get paid. Decide which day you want to communicate as the "public" Day One (i.e., the day you are introduced to your new organization) to facilitate other choices about order and location. Timing also counts when you are scheduling any virtual meetings with stakeholders in different time zones. Be mindful not to exclude people or require them to participate at inconvenient times.

Scheduling matters. It is very easy for Day One to quickly run off course. Use a calendar and plan your entire day out in 30-minute increments. This is not a time for lackadaisical planning.

Don't Stop at Day One: There is a good chance that everything you'd like to achieve won't all fit into Day One. Use the aforementioned Day One approach throughout your first week.

Tool 3.1 provides a convenient checklist for thinking about these things.

Make Careful Choices about Your Day One Plan

Using the preceding guidelines and your knowledge gained during your fuzzy front end, you will be well positioned to start planning your Day One. Look for indications of what actions might be especially effective and powerful, and work those items into your agenda.

Many have found value in holding early meetings with as many of the people in their organization as they can muster—in person, by videoconference, by teleconference, or the like. These early meetings give all a chance to lay their eyes on you. It does matter what you say in these meetings, but chances are that most people will not remember much beyond hello . . . unless you make a mistake. If they do remember, they'll probably remember the things you wish you'd never said. So, a safe option is to keep it simple, "Hello. I'm excited to be here and to start learning from you all" and not much else at this point.

Another valuable tool is the New Leader Assimilation Session. There is a template for this at the end of this chapter (Tool 3.2). It is easy to deploy and effective in bringing out all the questions that everyone really wants to ask in a forum where a critical mass can hear what you have to say, all at the same time. This prevents person A from filtering the message to person B, who filters it again, and so on.

There will always be rumors. But this process, originally created by Lynn Ulrich of the Wilfred Jarvis Institute and deployed in great depth at General Electric (GE), goes a long way toward squelching most of the rumors, innuendos, and misinformation. Hence, do this as early in your tenure as possible, preferably Day One. The session works in multiple scenarios, including new leaders entering new roles, as well as for new owners in the early days following an acquisition or a new investment by a private equity firm.

The New Leader Assimilation model can be adapted for Day One/Early Days in an acquisition integration scenario. More on New Owner Assimilation and other tools and approaches appears in Chapter 12.

Don't Reinvent the Wheel: Start with This Prototypical Agenda

Although no two executives' Day Ones are ever the same, it's often easier to start with a model. Yes, you can ratchet up others' best current thinking as well as your own.

You can use the following sample agenda as a guideline for crafting your own Day One:

- Early-morning meeting with your boss to reconfirm and update
- Meet and greet over coffee, juice, or the like with broad group to say hello (and not much more)
- One-on-one meetings as appropriate
- New Leader's Assimilation (Tool 3.2) with direct reports and their direct reports
- Afternoon activity/meetings/walkabout to reinforce key message by living your message instead of talking about it
- End-of-day cocktails/coffee/social for more informal greetings
- Courtesy notes, voicemail for thank-you or follow-up, where needed and appropriate
- Brief communication with your boss or board member to begin the habit of staying connected, as appropriate

Perhaps the best way to get across the power of a well-planned Day One is through examples of others' Day One experiences.

What Not to Do on Day One

A new chief customer officer was hired by a new CEO.

The outgoing chief customer officer had taken charge of his replacement's onboarding plan. Interestingly, he had built a plan that had the new chief customer officer:

- Being announced to everyone (including customers) via a press release
- Focusing his attention on a segment of the business that represented only 8% of the total business
- Meeting no customers in his first month—none

It sure seemed as if the outgoing chief customer officer was setting his predecessor up for failure to make himself look good by comparison. Fortunately, we were able to redirect things before the chief customer officer's start.

Don't give up control of your own Day One. Do look for insight from your boss and possibly human resources but push back if it doesn't match with your going in message. Remember, everything communicates.

Some other watchouts:

- Don't get captured by the wrong people. (Per the previous story, not everyone may have your best interests at heart.)

- Don't use a PowerPoint presentation to introduce yourself. No one cares about you as their primary concern. They do care about what your presence means for them. Everyone has one and only one question: "What does this mean for me?"

- Don't tell too much information about your personal life. When in doubt, reread the previous bullet point.

- Don't say anything (good or bad) about your former company. It just raises questions about why you're not still there.

- Don't say anything negative about anybody in your new company.

- Don't schedule a doctor's appointment.

- Don't leave to look for an apartment or home.

- Don't show up late.

- Don't have lunch meetings with former colleagues.

- Don't consume alcohol at lunch.

- Don't tell anything but the mildest joke. You can't be too careful here.

- Don't share your political opinions.

- Don't spend excessive time on the phone setting up logistics for your move.

- Don't dress inappropriately.

- Don't decorate your office.

- Don't panic if things go awry.

HOT TIP

Manage Day One: Even though everything communicates, some communication is more important than others. How you spend Day One leaves an indelible impression. Control the agenda, even if you have to redefine which day is Day One.

HOT TIP

Day One is a critical part of **assimilation**. Welcome and get help from HR in terms of getting started working with others. Assimilation is a big deal. Doing it well makes things far easier. Getting it wrong triggers relationship risks. There are a couple of things beyond basic orientation that can make a huge difference. Encourage HR or others to set up onboarding conversations for you with members of your formal and informal/shadow networks. Ask HR or others to do periodic check-ins with those networks. If there are issues, you want to know about them early, so you can adjust.

Summary and Implications

At the start of a new role, everything is magnified. Thus, it is critical to be particularly thoughtful about everything you do and say and don't do and don't say . . . and what order you do or say them in.

As you plan your own Day One, here are a couple of things to keep in mind:

- *It is personal.* As a leader, you impact people's lives. Those people will try very hard to figure out you and your potential impact as soon as they can. They may even rush to judgment. Keep that in mind at all times.

- *Order counts.* Be circumspect about the order in which you meet with people and the timing of when you do what throughout Day One and your early days.

- *Messages matter.* Have a message. Know what you are going to say and not say. Have a bias toward listening. Know that strong opinions, long-winded introductions, and efforts to prove yourself immediately are rarely, if ever, good Day One tactics. People will be looking to form opinions early. Keep that in mind while deciding when to listen, when to share, what to ask, whom to ask, and how you answer. When speaking, keep it brief, on point, congenial, and meaningful.

- *Location counts*. Think about where you will show up for work on Day One. Do not just show up at your designated office by default.

- *Signs and symbols count*. Be aware of all the ways you communicate, well beyond your words.

- *Timing counts*. Day One does not have to match the first day you get paid. Decide which day you want to communicate as Day One to facilitate other choices about order and location.

- *Scheduling counts*. Plan your Day One in 30-minute increments.

QUESTIONS YOU SHOULD ASK YOURSELF

What am I doing on Day One? Where am I doing it? What does it communicate?

Am I being thoughtful about all the ways I am communicating on Day One?

Am I making the impression I want to make on the people I choose to make it on?

What might people want to know, and how will I answer the questions should I be asked?

What is my message and does my Day One agenda support it?

Note the most up-to-date, full, editable versions of all tools are downloadable at primegenesis.com/tools.

TOOL 3.1
Day One Plan

Official Day One:

Effective Day One:

Your Message:

Your Entry Plan (detailed, calendared)

Initial Large-Group Meetings:

Initial Small-Group Meetings:

New Leader Assimilation Date:

Other Internal Stakeholder Meetings:

External Stakeholder Meetings:

External Stakeholder Phone Calls:

Meals—Breakfast, Lunch, Dinner:

Walking Around Time:

Message in Action: An activity that communicates your message. Be. **Do**. Say. (Live or virtually)

End-of-Day Thank You Notes/Calls:

TOOL 3.2
New Leader Assimilation

The Ulrich/GE new leader assimilation process gets questions on the table and resolved immediately that would fester without it. This is a useful session to conduct in the first days or weeks of a new leadership role.

STEP 1: Provide a brief introduction and an overview of the objectives of the session, and review the process to all involved (team and new leader).

STEP 2: Team members, without the new leader present, generate questions about:

1. The new leader (you).

(Questions may concern, e.g., professional profile or personal hopes, dreams, rumors, preconceptions, concerns.)

(continued)

TOOL 3.2   New Leader Assimilation (continued)

2. The new leader as a team leader.

   (Questions may concern what the leader knows about, e.g., the team, priorities, work style, norms, communication, rumors.)

3. The new leader as a member of the broader organization.

   (Questions may concern what the leader knows about, e.g., the organization, how they fit, priorities, assumptions, expectations, rumors.)

   The team should also answer the following questions that they'll present to the new leader:

4. What does the new leader need to know to be successful in the new role?

   What are the top three issues?

   What are the secrets to being effective? Are there any ideas for the new leader?

5. What significant issues need to be addressed immediately? Are there any quick fixes that are needed now?

   Are there any difficult areas of the business that the new leader should know about?

6. Other questions and ideas?

   What is the one question that you are afraid to ask? What additional messages do you have?

STEP 3: New leader rejoins team to answer questions, listen, and learn.

Note: For remote teams, a facilitator can gather questions and comments from the group in advance, synthesize, and prioritize key topics and then pose them to the leader on a group video call.

CHAPTER 4

Evolve the Culture.
Leverage Diversity

	Converge			Pivot		Evolve		
	Day One			30	45	60	70	100

| Position Yourself for success | Leverage the Fuzzy Front End | Take control of Day One | Lay your Leadership Foundation | Co-create Burning Imperative | Embed Milestone Management | Invest in Early Wins | Realign Team | Adjust and Advance |

L eaders inspire, enable, and empower others to do their absolute best together to realize a meaningful and rewarding shared purpose. But to be a great leader, you must know why people follow you, what you should do, and how you can help those following you. Because leadership, culture, and communications are inextricably linked, these next two chapters will tackle all three as you lay the foundation of your leadership to bridge tactical capacity into your team.

"They can because they think they can." —Virgil

The goal is to build a self-confident team. You can elicit self-confidence in your team by delegating and building trust in four areas:

1. **Direction.** Providing direction helps others follow. Start with the problem you need solved or the opportunity you can seize.

69

Be clear on *what* they should accomplish. Then, let them determine *how* to get it done. Finally, seed self-confidence by empowering them to do it their way within appropriate guidelines or
strategic boundaries.

2. **Authority.** It's counterintuitive to some, but bounded authority
   is more confidence-building than is blanket authority. Strategic
   boundaries for tactical decisions give people confidence in their
   ability to make those tactical decisions without worrying about
   others second-guessing them.

3. **Resources.** Instead of giving them the resources *you* think they
   need, ask them what *they* think they need. Then, help them
   assemble those resources or make things work with the
   resources available.

4. **Accountability.** Assume they will succeed. Have confidence in
   the people to whom you delegate. Show them your confidence
   in them and in their approach. Recognize and reward them for
   their achievements at milestone steps along the way to bring out
   their self-confidence.

Putting it all together. If you're lucky enough to have followed a
confidence-activating pinnacle executive, you know how it feels.[1] You
know how it feels to follow someone who cares about building enduring greatness, puts others first, and is relentless in the pursuit of what
matters. You know how it feels to follow someone who lives "Be. Do.
Say." Someone you respect for who they are and what they represent.
You know how it feels to follow someone who trusts you, makes you
feel better about yourself, and brings out your own self-confidence.

Intentionally Evolve the Culture

At this point you've already leveraged your fuzzy front end to learn
quickly, you've refined your plans along the way, you've developed solid
relationships with all your key stakeholders, and you've got a leadership progression plan in place for you and your team. You made a
strong early impression by delivering a clear message to your new

---

[1] George Bradt, 2019, "How Great Leaders Bring Out Others' Self-Confidence,"
Forbes, November 5.

audiences (up, down, and across) that reflects the platform for change and the calls to action for your team. Your team is engaged.

You've also determined your leadership approach by deciding whether you were going to assimilate, converge and evolve quickly, converge and evolve slowly, or shock the system. You've acknowledged what you need to do differently, behaviorally, to become a pinnacle leader in this situation.

Whatever your chosen course, now is the time to turn your attention to the culture. By now, your insights on the culture are probably sharper than when you started. You are now able to start to *intentionally* evolve the culture.

In fact, it's essential. Do not skip this step. One of the biggest mistakes new leaders make is to either forget about the culture or assume it will just casually evolve to some undefined but desired utopia. If you want the culture to evolve (you do!) and be a positive, deeply embedded powerful force driving the team toward its goals (you do!) that creates engaged stakeholders who feel valued and committed to the cause (you do!), then you must act with clear intention.

The BRAVE framework allows a relatively easy, robust assessment of culture and character by looking at behaviors, relationships, attitudes, values, and the environment. Cross this with "Be. Do. Say." While words matter, people's actions often don't match their words. And even if their actions do match their words but not their fundamental, underlying beliefs, they will eventually be exposed. As former Goldman Sachs CEO Lloyd Blankfein told the *New York Times'* Andrew Ross Sorkin, "the character thing in the long run always came out at the worst possible time."[2]

Look beyond the behaviors, relationships, attitudes, values, and environment an individual or society presents as its public face to discover what's really going on. Some define character or culture as what you believe, think, say, and do when no one is listening or watching.

The good news is that we have a simple three-part process that will kickstart your cultural evolution:

1. **Define the current state:** Start by articulating the current values and guiding principles that the organization (your team)

---

[2] Andrew Ross Sorkin and Ephrat Livni, "When Business and Politics Mix, 'Character Really Counts,'" *New York Times* (January 9, 2021).

has been operating under. Keep in mind that every organization has defined and undefined cultural elements. Look for both. It's important at this stage to also capture any negative aspects of the current culture. At this point, there are almost certainly aspects of the culture that you have yet to experience. So don't do this alone. Culture is always a team sport. You can come in with a solid perspective to jump-start discussions, but you must engage the team as a group to get an accurate and complete picture of the current state. Next, use the BRAVE culture assessment tool (modified with different subdimensions so it works for your situation) to help you document and articulate the current state.

2. **Define the desired destination:** Next, co-create the elements of your new, aspirational culture by engaging a broad set of people (up, down, and across) throughout the organization. Have broad meaningful conversations with the team to discuss important values, guiding principles, and required behaviors. Ask the team: What's working? What's not working? What should we keep doing? What should we start doing? What should we stop doing? Always keep in mind that you want to evolve the culture to a place where it will help you compete and win. Define who you want to be. Use Tool 4.1 to augment these conversations and evaluate where you are as an organization against the dimensions of a BRAVE culture compared with where you want to be. Record a current state and a desired state for each aspect of each component.

3. **Create your culture evolution roadmap:** You can't change the culture overnight. Don't try it; it never works. Instead, choose the most important elements that you want to shift first and decide what behaviors and practices must be changed to produce the desired evolution. This is a good time to refine the answers to the keep, stop, and start questions you asked earlier. Reinforce the consistent communication and be sure to recognize and reward behaviors and practices that support the new desired state. Consider this a multi-phased approach. As you see the culture shift on the first set of elements you chose to evolve, move on, and work on the next most important elements. As this plan evolves, you will be creating and maintaining a winning culture that will become your greatest competitive advantage.

Your desired culture destination and your culture evolution road-map will change as you continue to learn and as the team gets tightly aligned around future business direction. Make note to adjust the culture destination and culture evolution roadmap after the team has co-created its future focus in the burning imperative workshop.

Culture-Shaping Tools

Now that you've got your roadmap in place, there are many tools available to help you evolve your culture. Here are several that can make the greatest impact.

Performance Feedback and Reviews

Adapt your performance feedback and review process in a couple ways. First, in the formal written process, be sure to include not only "business" goals that can be measured but also force an evaluation (including a numeric value) on the stated company behaviors and values. Make sure the process includes inputs from multiple stakeholders to provide a well-rounded perspective. When providing feedback in this forum, be detailed and specific. Go out of your way to provide specific examples of "culture-enhancing" behaviors as well as "culture-killing" behaviors.

Informally, model a culture where constructive feedback is given and received in the spirit of individual and company improvement. Be ready to give feedback—both negative and positive—in the moment.

Reward and Recognition

Think of reward and recognition as the public version of positive feedback. Deploy a simple program that recognizes not only performance against business goals but also demonstration of culture-enhancing behaviors and values. At first, control the process so managers get a feel for what is deserving of recognition. Once you are confident the program will be applied consistently, allow managers and employees to recognize their peers and coworkers. More positive feedback will lead to more positive behaviors!

Communication

An active internal communications program is the lifeblood of a cultural evolution. First, get your messages clear, what you wish to reinforce about the culture you are driving. If people need to work more closely as a team to solve customer problems, institute a Lunch & Learn or similar program to share information and get on the same page. Or encourage leadership team members to invite peers to their staff meeting to share news from their departments. If you are trying to evolve the team and the culture to a more aggressive posture in the market, celebrate wins examples where team members were assertive, took a risk, and won the business.

Additional Tools and Processes

The following are covered in detail in later chapters and are worth highlighting here for a holistic array of tools and processes to help shape your culture in line with your organizational objectives:

> *Burning imperative workshop:* session for the team to co-create and align around its mission, vision, values, goals, strategies, and big block action plans for results.

> *Milestone management:* a process that embeds accountability and collaboration within the team to achieve milestones and goals.

> *Early wins:* a process and mindset to overinvest in delivering results as a means to build momentum and team confidence, in themselves, in you as leader, and in the shared imperative.

> *Role sort:* an opportunity to step back and determine if you have the right roles on your team, and the right players in those roles, in order to achieve your business and cultural objectives.

> *Adjustment:* a process to assess your own progress against previous expectations, gain stakeholder feedback, and make course corrections in areas of focus and leadership approach.

Leverage Diversity, Embed Equity, and Foster Inclusion

Diversity, equity, and inclusion (DE&I) should not be a scary or third rail topic for any leader. Rather, it belongs as a fundamental priority for the leadership team. To some extent, the concept has been high-jacked by various groups who want to push their talking points without any practical understanding of leadership or how to build a high-performing, diverse, and equitable team. Ironically, so much of the noise around this powerful part of team building has moved it from a fun, joyous leadership responsibility and culture-driving enabler to a threatening numbers-based topic. Tune out those who seek to divide and turn your focus and attention to ways in which you can unite. That's what you do as a leader.

As a leader you should think of DE&I not as a "program" but as a mindset or a foundational element of the culture. Once it is, you'll be embracing and practicing DE&I without even knowing it. For many, especially the younger generations, how a company responds to and treats its people will have a direct impact on recruiting, retention, engagement, and trust. Those who do it well will have a significant competitive advantage over those who don't do it well. Leveraging diversity, embedding equity, and fostering inclusion will help you build a winning culture that accelerates achievement of your mission, vision, and goals.

DE&I is not just a number. It's not achieved by just hitting a quota. It's not an HR-only benchmark. It doesn't exist because a written policy has been added to the employee handbook, and it doesn't just happen because you've added it to your core values. Numbers and policies are important, but those alone won't achieve the goal. You'll need to add action and accountability from the top down, bottom up, and middle out if you're really going to be able to take advantage of the benefits of greater diversity, equity, and inclusion.

Like many topics in this book, we don't have enough space to fully discuss this topic, and like so many issues it will be something that you will want to continually work on for as long as you are a leader of anything. For now, let's look at what you can do to embed DE&I into your culture in a meaningful and powerful way.

Leverage Diversity

Think about diversity as differences that exist between people. Diversity can exist between race, religion, sexual orientation, ethnicity, nationality, age, political opinion, socioeconomic disability versus abilities, and language, to name a few. It boils down to perspective based on different experiences. We are all different in so many ways from each other, and as such we come to situations with a diversity of perspectives.

Julie Sweet, the CEO of Accenture, says: "We believe our diversity makes us stronger, smarter, and more innovative, helping us better serve the needs of our clients, our people and our communities."

Embed Equity

Equity is about being fair and impartial in your people, plans, and practices and the culture that supports them. It ensures that everyone has equal access.

Abraham Lincoln said, "These men ask for just the same thing, fairness, and fairness only. This, so far as in my power, they, and all others, shall have."

Foster Inclusion

Inclusion is about enabling people to feel invited, included, and welcomed because their voices are not only acknowledged but also heard. Everyone has a sense of belonging, value, and respect.

Claudia Brind-Woody, vice president and managing director for global intellectual property licensing at IBM, says, "Inclusivity means not just 'we're allowed to be there,' but 'we are valued.' I've always said: smart teams will do amazing things, but truly diverse teams will do impossible things."

A Starting Point

A common phrase you'll hear about DE&I is that diversity is being invited to the dance, whereas equity is equal access to space on the dance floor and input on the music being played, and inclusion is being asked to dance. Good leaders will create environments that leverage and value different perspectives; embed equal access and opportunities to all; and foster a sense of belonging, value, and respect.

Whether you decide to engage the culture by assimilating, converging and evolving, or shocking, please recognize that in almost all scenarios you'll want to pay close attention to DE&I to ensure that leveraging, embedding, and fostering becomes core to the culture. Achieving true DE&I is a special challenge and requires a thoughtful approach to understand what's really going on, how you converge and adapt, and how you influence change. Dr. Gregory Pennington wrote a chapter in *Influence and Impact*[3] on how to think about and deal with bias and discrimination in the workplace with a framework of five considerations: calibration, information, demonstration, negotiation, and transformation. Paraphrasing that for you as a new leader:

1. **Calibration**

    The primary emphasis in calibration is to find a way to validate what you are experiencing and may experience by comparing it with other reference points. These include other experiences of your own and comparisons to experiences of others. It is primarily an internal process and provides a foundation for the other areas of focus. The power of calibration is in how it influences your framing of the situation and your personal responsibility for it.

2. **Information**

    The focus on information emphasizes the importance of gathering additional sources of data and broadening the context of your experiences. It also provides perspective about individual, leader, and organization patterns and impacts. It is a shift from a primarily internal process to one that is external in its accumulation of data and in its sharing of data. The power of information is in how and with whom you share it.

3. **Demonstration**

    The focus on demonstration is an emphasis on proving you and others can perform at the levels expected by the organization. It is also an effort to eliminate the possibility that others and the organization can use failure to perform as a justification for discrimination based on that variable. Demonstration is an external process, and its power is convincing yourself and others that you and others are willing to be judged on the essential need of the organization to deliver results.

4. **Negotiation**

    The emphasis of negotiation is leveraging the areas of calibration, information, and demonstration to align what the

---

[3] Bill Berman and George Bradt, 2021, *Influence and Impact: Discover and Excel at What Your Organization Needs from You the Most*, Hoboken, NJ: John Wiley & Sons.

organization needs and wants with what you and others need and want. It is clearly an external process and certainly an interactive one. The power of this area of focus is in connecting changes in behavior to observable outcomes.

5. **Transformation**

Transformation represents the fifth area of focus and emphasizes the opportunity for you as a leader to change others and the organization. It takes advantage of the degrees of influence accumulated through the previous stages. As both an internal and external process, it derives its power from you being genuinely committed to changing others, being in a position of interpersonal and organizational influence to do so, and effectively engaging others in the process.

If you apply this framework to the strategic, operational, and organizational processes in your enterprise, you'll see that diversity, equity, and inclusion are most impactful when embedded in your culture. Beware, this is not a one-time exercise, but a continual deployment of all five considerations across all aspects of the organization. That may sound overwhelming, but with repetition and practice it can become a foundational element of your culture.

In your first 100 days as a leader, you can take a few simple steps to make a start in building a culture that embraces diversity, equity, and inclusion:

1. **Know current policies.** Engage immediately. Familiarize yourself with current DE&I policies and cultural norms. Improve them where they are lacking.

2. **Get the facts.** Understand the reality of your current situation relative to diversity hiring, development and promotions compared with stated policies and goals, and capture observations about how inclusive (or not) decision-making and other key processes really are in the organization.

3. **Set the tone.** In your communication and especially your actions, make it clear that you value DE&I and that it will be an integral part of the organization. Note that empathy and compassion are essential. Most importantly, demonstrate it in all your actions. Make it clear that people can expect to express themselves and be heard regardless of their gender, religion, ethnicity, sexual orientation, political opinion, age, and so forth.

4. **Engage HR.** Partner with HR to enhance, improve, and instill behaviors and principles that will leverage, embed, and foster a DE&I culture.

5. **Build awareness of the benefits.** Talk about, discuss, and celebrate the benefits of a solid DE&I policy. Educate your team on how a DE&I culture enhances the organization's brand, innovation, creativity, recruiting, retention, happiness, and so forth.

6. **Communicate, encourage, and embrace differences.** Foster discussions. Value differences. Facilitate better solutions. Foster inclusion and collaboration. Make sure communication is respectful and open.

7. **Encourage, empower, and help your team.** Talk to everyone about DE&I. Ask them what and how they think about it. Do they need help? What resources do they need? Make sure every team member has a stake in the process.

8. **Begin to build the culture.** Take the time to build a diverse, equitable, and inclusive culture through targeted policies and practices around talent acquisition, development, and succession planning.

9. **Create accountability.** Measure individual performance and team results against DE&I goals.

To create or be a part of a culture that leverages diversity, embeds equity, and fosters inclusion, lay the foundation of a DE&I culture by taking the previous steps early on. You won't get anywhere near the top two levels of aforementioned leadership without doing so. Remember, it's not just numbers, quotas, or checklist. It must be deeply engrained in the culture. If you fail to create a culture that values DE&I, there's an almost certain chance you'll fail as a leader in today's world. Work hard on this one. It's worth the effort. Succeed and you'll feel better about yourself, your team, and the world in general.

Summary and Implications

- **Leaders inspire, enable, and empower.** Focus on bringing out self-confidence in others by how you delegate and build trust across (1) direction, (2) bounded authority, (3) resources, and (4) accountability.

- **Be intentional** about setting a path toward your desired target culture and what you will do differently as a leader to influence the change.

- **Diversity, equity, and inclusion** should be embedded in your culture. You'll need to add action and enforce accountability from the top down, bottom up, and middle out if you're really going to be able to take advantage of the benefits that leveraging diversity, embedding equity, and fostering inclusion will bring.

QUESTIONS YOU SHOULD ASK YOURSELF

Am I clear on my own leadership approach?

Am I clear about what I need to do differently, behaviorally, to support that approach?

Am I clear on the target culture and its next evolutionary step?

Are others equally clear on where we are headed and why?

Are we making concrete, practical progress on diversity, equity, and inclusion?

How are we *leveraging* diversity on our team?

How are we *fostering* inclusion?

How are we *embedding* equity?

Note the most up-to-date, full, editable versions of all tools are downloadable at primegenesis.com/tools.

TOOL 4.1
Culture Evolution Road Map

	Destination		
	Dimension 1	Dimension 2	Dimension 3

KEEP

How we lead

How we get work done

(processes and procedures)

How we interact

How we communicate
(two-way)

BOOST

How we lead

How we get work done

(processes and procedures)

How we interact

How we communicate
(two-way)

ELIMINATE

How we lead

How we get work done

(processes and procedures)

How we interact

How we communicate
(two-way)

CHAPTER 5

Manage Communication, Especially Digitally with Your Remote Team

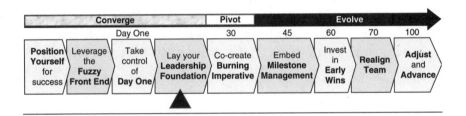

E verything communicates. Everything—even the things you don't do and don't say send powerful signals to everybody in the organization observing you.

Because we live amid a communication revolution, the guidelines for communicating are changing dramatically. As much as you would like to treat communication as a logical, sequential, ongoing communication campaign, in many cases, you must manage it as an iterative set of concurrent conversations.

The prescription for communication during the time between Day One and co-creating a burning imperative requires discipline and finesse for the new leaders following this program. The time before co-creating a burning imperative is all about converging—almost always.

This means you can't launch your full-blown communication efforts yet. You can't stand up and tell people your new ideas. If you do, they are your ideas, and not the team's ideas.

So, this period leading up to co-creating a burning imperative is marked by a lot of listening and learning. Your learning will be directed by your message. You'll be living your message, but you're most definitely not launching a communication campaign of any sort.

Keep that in mind as you go through the rest of this chapter, which lays out some points on communication that you may or may not start during this period but will certainly use later.

Where to Start and What You Need to Know

Before activating your ongoing communication efforts after Day One, you'll need to address several key components, each of which is essential. As a foundation to your approach, per Chapter 2 and before launch, you should have done the following:

1. Identified your *target audience*
2. Crafted an *overarching message*
3. Determined the *key communication points*

This is a good time to take a stop and rethink each of these elements given what you have learned and make any adjustments so they accurately reflect your current best thinking.

Use Your Communication to Drive Engagement

There's an ever-strengthening body of evidence that engaged employees produce better results.[1] Engagement is too important and dynamic a metric to live with a binary distinction between the engaged and unengaged. Instead, think of engagement in terms of four levels: committed, contributors, watchers, and detractors.

---

[1] Steve Crabtree, 2013, "Worldwide, 13% of Employees Are Engaged at Work," Gallup, October 8.

Committed: The committed are driven by the purpose, the cause, and doing good for others. They believe and will do whatever it takes to accomplish the desired results. Keep them committed with simple direct communication that touches their emotions and gets them to believe viscerally in what you're trying to do together.

Contributors: The contributors are good at what they do and it shows. They enjoy their work. Their output is positive and helps keep moving the ball down the field. They are important players, but not necessarily leaders. Communicate with them directly so they understand what is required of them.

Watchers: The watchers are compliant and primarily driven by what is good for them and concerned about their basic needs. Compliant people aren't hurting the organization, but they are not primary drivers of change. They are doing what they are told and no more. The goal is to make them aware of what they need to do and make sure it gets done.

Detractors: The detractors are disengaged and have checked out emotionally. They don't believe in the platform for change, the vision, or the call to action. They won't do what the organization needs them to do. Their complete disconnect qualifies them as detractors. If they don't immediately respond to the new messaging, move them out, quickly.

Consider What Drives Happiness

People on your team want to be happy. Everyone finds happiness by some combination of:

1. Doing good for others
2. Doing things, they are good at
3. Doing good for themselves

In the work environment, the committed are motivated by all three elements and therefore are usually among the happiest team members. The contributors are motivated by elements two and three, and the compliant are motivated by element three. Sadly, the disengaged are not finding happiness in any element.

Different people are motivated more by one bucket than by another. The more focused someone is on doing good for others, the more likely that the other elements of happiness fall into place as well. Mother Theresa was almost exclusively focused on doing good for others; while she did that, she became very good at what she did, and her work was also good for her. Great artists, such as cellist Yo-Yo Ma, may not care about the impact they make on others or their own rewards; they just want to pursue their art for the sake of the art, because it brings them joy to do what they are good at. Some Hollywood producers and actors are driven more by doing what's good for themselves, money and fame, rather than the quality of the films they create.

Maslow's Needs

The core of Maslow's theory is that there is a hierarchy of needs.[2] At the bottom, people must satisfy their physiological and safety needs. With those in place, they can move on to belonging and esteem. Then, ultimately, they can tackle needs for self-actualization.

Add Maslow's hierarchy to the happiness and engagement frameworks, mix in a little communication planning, and out pops an approach that weaves all three together (Table 4.1).

Table 4.1
Communication Engagement Levels

Needs (Maslow)	Happiness Driver	Communication Approach	Communication Result	Engagement Level
Self-actualization	Good for others	Emotional	Belief	Committed
Belonging/ Esteem	Good at it	Direct	Understanding	Contributing
Physiological/ Safety	Good for me	Indirect	Awareness	Compliant

---

[2] Abraham H. Maslow, 1943, "A Theory of Human Motivation," *Psychological Review* 50(4): 370–96.

Satisfaction

The late Fredrick Herzberg was one of the first psychologists whose research focused heavily on business management. He was widely known for his two-factor theory on employee motivation in the workplace. According to Herzberg, the two components that drove satisfaction were hygiene factors and motivation factors. Hygiene is probably not what you're thinking. But let's not fault Herzberg for a poor choice of words. In his theory, job dissatisfaction was influenced by hygiene factors while job satisfaction was influenced by motivating factors.

The hygiene factors were considered things like company policies, supervisor quality, working conditions, salary, status, coworker relations, and security. The hygiene factors need to be good enough not to dissatisfy people. But there are severely diminished returns to taking them beyond good enough.

The motivating factors were considered things like achievement, recognition, the work itself, responsibility, advancement, and growth. Improving these factors increased job satisfaction. The more they were increased the better the satisfaction.

Maslow Hygiene and Motivating Factors

In general, the first two levels of Maslow's hierarchy are hygiene factors. People's physiological and safety needs need to be met well enough for them not to be problems. The top levels are motivating factors. The more self-esteem and self-actualization, the better.

Belonging benefits are caught in the middle. They are higher-level than hygiene factors, but often not motivators on their own. People want to belong to a club, tribe, or fan base—but it matters only if that membership builds their self-esteem or self-actualization.

Implications for You as a Leader

Those you lead are always going to be evolving. This is especially true after a crisis or a rapid shift in circumstances like the rapid and massive move to remote work when everyone's progress up Maslow's hierarchy of physiological, safety, belonging, self-esteem, and self-actualization slips or stalls.

When that happens, you need to reboot your relationships with them. Meet them where they are in Maslow's hierarchy. Fighting that is like fighting the tide. You'll lose.

Align the way you influence with their shifted attitudes on work–life balance, health and wellness, relationship, place in the world, and other things. Then, help them move back up Maslow's hierarchy to where they were or beyond.

Become the Narrator-in-Chief

Allen Schoer, the founder and chair of the leadership consultancy TAI Group, has an interesting take on the power of stories. He suggests that:

- Stories yield narrative.
- Narrative yields meaning.
- Meaning yields alignment.
- Alignment yields performance.

Stories matter if you choose the right ones. With the right stories, you can influence but not control those committed to the cause. But you are not going to be the only one telling the stories that communicate the message. Others are going to tell their own stories in their own ways. So, you're not the only storyteller, but you can be the narrator-in-chief, guiding others to choose stories that are in line with the core message.

Touch Points

Touch points are moments at which your target audiences are *touched* or reached by your message. Effective communication must include multiple touch points in multiple venues. Determine both the number of people you reach and the frequency with which you touch them. For the key individuals and groups that you want to touch, map out a series of media methods to do so, including face-to-face conversations, phone calls, videoconferences, notes, e-mails, texts, and more general mass and social media communications.

Monitor and Adjust

You are going to lose control of the communication as soon as you start. As people relate what they've heard to others, they will apply their own filters and biases. Shame on you if you're not ready for that and have not considered DE&I. Have a system in place to monitor how your message is being translated. Be ready to capitalize on opportunities and head off issues that could derail your momentum. Although you can't prepare for every eventuality, if you think through a range of scenarios, you're more likely to use those contingency plans as a starting point for your response. Determine how you will measure the success of the message. Just getting it out to the audience does not mean that you've been successful. Be sure you know how and at what frequency you will measure whether your message is being received as intended.

Repeat the Message Repeat the Message

In your communication efforts, repetition is essential. We'll say it again; repetition is essential. In other words, you're going to have to create different ways and times to repeat the same message over and over again. You'll get bored of your own message well before the critical mass has internalized it, but don't shy away from repeating it. Do not ever let your boredom show; make sure you keep your energy and excitement levels high regarding the message. When you're done, do it again, fitting it into the right context for each audience each time.

Celebrate Early Wins

Somewhere along the way, you will have identified an early win for your first six months. As part of this campaign, you will have overinvested to deliver that win. When it is complete, celebrate it, and celebrate it publicly. This is all about giving the team confidence in itself. So invest your time to make the team members feel great.

Reinforce

There is going to be a crisis of confidence at some point. At that point the team will question whether you're really serious about these changes and whether the changes you are making are going to stick. Be ready for the crisis and use that moment to reinforce your efforts.

The first thing you need is an early warning system to see the crisis developing. By this time, you should be able to tap other eyes and ears throughout the organization to get an on-the-street read of the situation. These are going to be people who feel safe telling you what's really going on. They might be administrative staff, those outside your direct line of reports, or people far enough removed from you that they don't feel threatened telling you the truth. Whoever they are, you need to identify them and cultivate them. You'll often find these in the "committed" group we discussed earlier.

The main sign of the impending crisis will be the naysayers or detractors raising their heads and their objections again or more boldly. It is likely they will go quiet during the period of initial enthusiasm after the launch of the burning imperative. But they will usually find it impossible to stay quiet forever. Their return to naysaying will be the first signs of the crisis, and their point of view will spread if you don't cut it off.

So hit the restart button fast. Make it clear that you are committed to the changes. Regroup your core team to confirm its commitment. Positively recognize the committed and contributor—those making an effort to drive the team change imperative. And take action against the blocking coalitions, with negative consequences ranging from feedback to moving people off the team if they are hindrances to business and cultural progress. Some good steps at this point may include:

- Regroup with your core team to gather input and adjust as appropriate.
- *All-hands* meetings, videoconferences, or calls to highlight progress and reinforce the burning imperative.
- Follow-up note confirming the commitment to the burning imperative.
- Follow-up phone calls with each individual on the core team.
- Reinforce the burning imperative at each key milestone with core team, their teams, and others.
- Meet or have one-on-ones with key people or groups at a level below your direct reports.

- Conduct field or plant visits.

- Implement a structured plan to measure the effectiveness of your communications.

- Introduce a reward and recognition program to reinforce strong performance and supporting behaviors.

HOT TIP

Think in terms of a network of communication: Discover your core message. Then use that to guide key communication points in an iterative set of concurrent conversations across a network of multiple stakeholders and a wide variety of mediums, all built on a foundation of trustworthy authenticity. Effective communication is hard work, but it will be one of the most important and most enduring things you do.

At Charley Shimanski's first conference as head of the American Red Cross's disaster response operations, he hosted 140 disaster response directors and other colleagues. It was a master class in communication. Charley was everywhere: on the stage introducing speakers, speaking himself, reconnecting with old friends, hugging people who had gone through tough response engagements. He owned the room and reinforced the attendees' passion for the cause. His message flowed from every action, every message, and every pore of his being.

When asked about how he prepared for a session like that, Charley explained that he doesn't think about what he's going to say and he doesn't think about what he wants his audience to hear. Instead, he thinks about how he wants them to feel.

"I wanted them to feel that they are at the core of what we do, that our success is on their shoulders. I wanted them to feel proud."

On one hand, not everyone has a cause as generally meaningful as the Red Cross's disaster response mission: *"Provide relief to victims of disasters and help people prevent, prepare for, and respond to emergencies."*

But you *do* have a cause that is meaningful to you and to the people you're leading. If it didn't matter, you wouldn't be there. Be. Do.

Say. Communicate the message in what you say. Communicate it in what you do. Make it your own. Do that and those following you will commit to it. You'll all feel proud.

Leading Remote or Hybrid Teams

Chances are that you'll be leading a remote or hybrid team (partially remote or part-time remote) at some point. The Covid pandemic forced a mass transition to remote work, but the trends toward remote had been significantly increasing for over a decade. The sudden explosion of remote work changed the landscape forever. Many employers have realized that employees don't need to be in the office all the time to be productive. They've also recognized that to recruit and retain people, a remote or hybrid option is essential. A study done by Mercer in early 2021 found that 70 percent of companies planned on adopting some sort of hybrid model.

Overwhelmingly, employees who have experience working remotely have enjoyed it and prefer it to office-based work. No commute, time savings, higher productivity, better work–life balance, and more time for loved ones and hobbies are just some of the benefits remote workers highlight. Many will no longer consider jobs where some remote work is not an option. It's been a trend for a long time, but now it's a new way of working that is pervasive and won't be going away.

Managing a remote team—whether they are remote, you're remote, or you both are—comes with some challenges that you'll have to navigate. Here are a few things that you will want to focus on.

Establish Rules of Engagement

If you've followed our advice up to this point, you may have already covered some of these points. You should inform or in some cases co-create with your team rules of engagement that define:

- What type of technologies will be used for what type of meetings? For example, we will use our company-approved video conferencing for our team meetings and one-on-ones. We will communicate urgent news via text messaging. We use our company-approved messaging app for ongoing team chat. You get the picture.

- Agree on availability. Not everyone is in the same time zone, and not everyone works the same hours.
- Decide on minimum frequency of contact.
- Create rules of conduct for videoconferencing. For example, everyone's camera must be on. Meetings start on time. Microphone is off unless you're talking. You must stay for the whole meeting. We always check-in with the team members that are remote first. We use the chat box and other text features to enable more participation.

In-Person Communication

Don't forget about this! In person communication is best for emotionally charged situations and building relationships and trust. You can leverage all five senses (sight, sound, touch, smell, taste.) Use it when it makes sense.

Deploy Both Synchronous and Asynchronous Communication

Leverage different ways of communicating with different people in different situations.

Synchronous communication is what takes place in real time between two people or a group of people. In-person meetings, videoconferencing, and phone calls are all examples of synchronous communication. Use this when you need immediate response, personal touch, when you want to make people feel part of a broader team, or when it's a short duration or less complex issues. It's great for brainstorming or in-depth and dynamic conversations, first-time meetings, sales engagements, celebrations, or rapid problem-solving. Have a clear objective in mind for this type of communication.

WARNING!

In a meeting in which some are in person and some are virtual, the virtual people's ability to contribute is limited as they miss the side conversations that might happen during the meeting and breaks.

Asynchronous communication is where one person provides information or data and there is a lag before the recipients receive it. E-mail, Slack, and Facebook are examples of asynchronous communication. Use this when you want to enable diverse input over time, when you're working across time zones, or when you want to give respondents time to think. Don't use this type of communication in times of urgency.

Make Time for Social Interactions

Be careful that your remote work environment doesn't become all about work, all the time. It is an easy trap to fall into, neglecting the typical social interactions that are the glue that bond teams and culture. Ron Friedman, a psychologist who specializes in human motivation, puts it this way: "Discussing things not related to work—sports, books, and family, for example, reveals shared interests, allowing people to connect in genuine ways, which yields closer friendships and better teamwork."[3]

Isolation, loneliness, and feelings of disconnection are real problems for the remote workers. Encourage social interactions to counteract those and encourage feelings of belonging. It will have a positive impact on employee engagement, happiness, culture, and DE&I to name a few benefits.

There are many ways to embed and encourage social interaction with your remote team. Reserve the first few minutes of every meeting for non-work-related updates. Reserve time for virtual office parties and encourage virtual office excursions, guest speakers, virtual lunches, and games. Get creative and have fun with this.

Implications for You

There is no going back to all-hands-on-deck office scenarios for most of us. You either evolve your culture and your leadership style to match the remote and hybrid work environments or risk quickly becoming obsolete.

---

[3] Ron Friedman, 2021, "5 Things High-Performing Teams Do Differently," *Harvard Business Review*, October 21.

You will need some in-person meetings for emotionally charged situations, to rebuild relationships, and to help recent joiners build initial relationships. You'll likely want to take advantage of people's newfound technical prowess to benefit from the efficiencies of some virtual meetings. It's hard to imagine anyone traveling great distances for one-hour follow-up meetings instead of jumping on a video.

And shame on you if you don't make better use of asynchronous work. Free your people up to be more in control of their own time, so they can get updates on demand and give you the benefit of their best thinking when and how they do their best thinking—not when and how it's most convenient for you.

Summary and Implications

- **Manage your communication with a focus on** phasing, stakeholders, and message, flexing for various audiences, adjusting as appropriate on an ongoing basis, and deploying an old-school logical, sequential communication campaign when appropriate—though expecting that to be the case less and less over time.

- **Encouraging and enabling the right remote work** can enable even more diverse input and others' time management choices.

QUESTIONS YOU SHOULD ASK YOURSELF

Am I modifying my messages for different audiences?

Am I clear what behaviors I want from my audience(s)?

Is the content of my message compelling?

Have I considered the optimal design (form, venue) for each specific communication?

Have I designed a means of evaluating the effectiveness of my communications?

Does my communication approach reach all the key stakeholders in the best way for each of them?

Are we encouraging the right remote work to enable even more diverse input and time management?

Am I effective in moving people up the curve to committed champions?

CHAPTER 6

Pivot to Strategy

Co-Create the Burning Imperative by Day 30.

Converge				Pivot		Evolve		
		Day One		30	45	60	70	100
Position Yourself for success	Leverage the Fuzzy Front End	Take control of Day One	Lay your Leadership Foundation	Co-create Burning Imperative	Embed Milestone Management	Invest in Early Wins	Realign Team	Adjust and Advance

You can control your schedule during the fuzzy front end—mostly because no one expects you to do anything. You probably can control your schedule on Day One or, at least, have a big influence on it—mostly because no one expects you to have thought it through as much as you will have after reading this book. You will have far less control over the rest of your first 100 days— because all sorts of people will be putting all sorts of demands on your time.

Conversely, carving out team-building time is going to be tough, but building a high-performing team, focused on a shared imperative, is essential. So make the time. This is the pivot point in your leadership.

Creating the Burning Imperative

On top of everything else you have to do, and all the other demands on your schedule, make the time to implement the building blocks of tactical capacity. The starting point, and indeed the foundation, is the burning imperative with its components of headline, mission, vision, values, objectives, goals, strategies, plans, and operating cadence. Experienced, successful leaders inevitably say that getting people aligned around a vision and values and focused on urgent business matters are the most important things they have to do—and often the most difficult during their first 100 days.

The burning imperative is a clear, sharply defined, intensely shared, and purposefully urgent understanding from all of the team members of what they are "supposed to do, now" and how this burning imperative works with the larger aspirations of the team and the organization.

A burning imperative is different from a shared purpose. The difference between the two is timing, intensity, and duration. The shared purpose drives the long term, whereas your burning imperative drives the next phase of activity, now, on the way to the long term.

The burning imperative should be reflected in a shorthand summary or headline—most likely containing a strong, action-oriented verb. Remember the Apollo 13 example of "Get these men home alive." Clear. Sharply defined. Intensely shared. Purposefully urgent. It trumps all petty concerns. It didn't replace the overall shared purpose of exploring the universe to increase man's knowledge. The burning imperative moves the team forward to that longer-term shared purpose. That's what you're aiming for.

We all saw the same thing in northern Chile in 2010 when 33 miners were trapped for 69 days 2,230 feet below the ground. Almost no one thought that the rescuers would ever retrieve the bodies, let alone pull them out alive. But after 17 days of being trapped underground without contact with anyone, the miners sent a message to the surface that they were all alive! Instantly, the burning imperative was set: "Get these men out alive!" No one had a plan on how to get it done when the burning imperative was set, but the rescue team, with help from people around the world, invented a way to get those men home safely. That is a burning imperative at work!

Burn Rubber on the Way to a Burning Imperative

The burning imperative drives the primary focus of the leadership team every day. More than any single other factor, this—and the operational processes that ensure its implementation—is what distinguishes highly successful teams from teams that flounder and fail. More than any other single factor, this is the key to surviving and thriving in and accelerating a complex transition. Teams with a clear burning imperative are more flexible in their actions and reactions because each individual team member is confident that their team members are heading in the same direction.

Not everyone agrees on how fast you should move to get this in place. The argument for stretching out this process is that the risks of picking the wrong burning imperative are greater than the risks of moving too slowly. There have certainly been cases where this has been true. If things are going well, there's less urgency to change things.

However, most leadership changes are triggers for meaningful strategic, operational, or organizational change. There is an expectation that you will be evolving the team in a new direction—or at least moving them in the same direction at a meaningfully faster pace. Failing to build momentum early can create problems of its own. If some negative factor intervenes before you have started to move forward (e.g., you lose a key customer or a vital team member leaves), you may fall into a debacle. We all have seen that the pace of change is accelerating as information flows more and more freely. In that environment, even if things are going well, competitors are going to converge rapidly on your position.

You need to move quickly, get moving, and adapt as appropriate. Get this in place by Day 30.

HOT TIP

The burning imperative: This is the centerpiece of tactical capacity. When people talk about getting everyone on the same page, this is that page. Use whatever methodology you would like to get it in place. But do be sure to get it in place and get buy-in early. In a hot landing when there is an acute need for the team members to act, it's imperative that they do so quickly. It is not that there are just diminishing returns to doing this after Day 30; there is an actual cliff. After Day 30, the sense of urgency dissipates almost immediately and things start slipping precariously. So you really need to do whatever it takes to get this done by Day 30. This is a big deal.

Core Focus

Before diving into the specific components of the burning imperative, it is worth stepping back to determine the core focus of your organization and how that will play out thematically across your strategic, operational, organizational, cultural, and leadership choices.

There are four primary areas of focus: design, production, delivery, or service. Most organizations do all four to one degree or another in addition to marketing and selling, which all must do. Determine what is your organization's core focus—the area in which it most needs to excel to compete and win. This is an important choice because everything aligns around and flows from that decision.

We're going to build this up step by step.

1. The four core focus areas map across stability–flexibility and independence–interdependence axes (Figure 6.1).

FIGURE 6.1   Core Focus

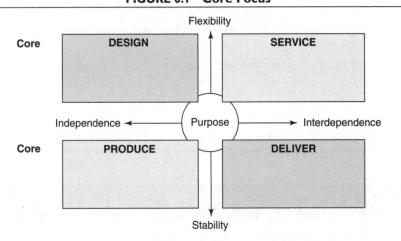

2. Each requires a different culture (Figure 6.2) with successful

   • Design-focused organization's cultures marked by learning and enjoyment in addition to independence and flexibility.

   • Production-focused organization's cultures marked by results and authority in addition to stability and independence.

   • Delivery-focused organization's cultures marked by order and safety in addition to *inter*dependence and stability.

FIGURE 6.2 Core Focus Culture

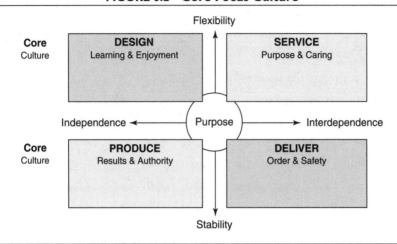

- Service-focused organization's cultures marked by purpose and caring in addition to flexibility and *inter*dependence.
3. Those cultures inform the organizations and operations (Figure 6.3) with
   - Specialized designers thriving with freeing support.
   - Hierarchical producers thriving with command and control.

FIGURE 6.3 Core Focus Organization and Operations

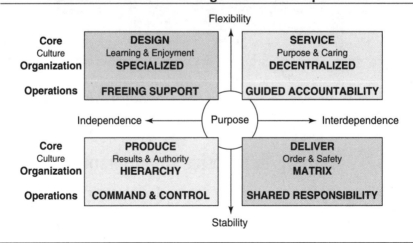

- Delivery systems that are inevitably matrices with shared responsibilities.
- The best service decisions made decentralized with guided accountability.

4. That means the leaders of

- Design-focused organizations need to enable with principles.
- Production-focused organizations need to enforce policies.
- Delivery-focused organizations need to enroll players across the ecosystem with team charters.
- Service-focused organizations need to be chief experience offers giving others guidelines (Figure 6.4).

FIGURE 6.4   Core Focus Full

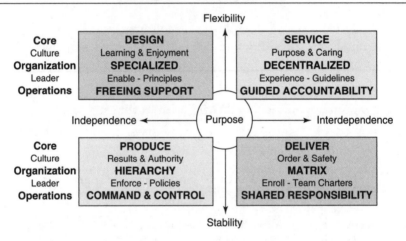

This is not a mix-and-match exercise. Once you identify your organization's core focus, things fall into place.

Burning Imperative Components

The components of the burning imperative are headline, mission, vision, values, objectives, goals, strategies, plans, and operating cadence. Together, these drive the team's actual plans and actions.

Headline: The all-encapsulating phrase or tagline that defines your burning imperative

Mission: *Why* are we here, what is our purpose

Vision: Future picture—*what* we want to become, where we are going, concrete picture of success

Values: Beliefs and moral principles that guide and underpin attitudes, relationships, and behaviors

Objectives: Broadly defined, qualitative performance requirements

Goals: The quantitative measures of the objectives that define success

Strategies: Broad choices around how the team will achieve its objectives, which should address:

> **Where to play** (products/services, geographies, channels, segments)
>
> **How to win** (initiatives to deliver success)
>
> **Capabilities** (knowledge, skills, technologies, processes to deliver strategic priorities)

Plans: Clarity on the what–who–when for programs that will bring each strategic priority to fruition

Operating cadence: How the team is going to implement, track, learn, and evolve plans, together

Ownership and accountability: Clearly defined choices about who does what, who is ultimately responsible, decision-making rights, bounded authority, and accountability

People often confuse the difference between a mission and a vision. Sometimes people just combine the two. But they are different. A mission guides what people do every day and why it matters. It informs what roles need to exist in the organization. A vision is the picture of *what* future success will look like. It helps define areas where the organization needs to be best in class and helps keep everyone aware of the essence of the company. *Best in class* means better than anyone else—superiority. *World-class* means in a class with the best— parity. Both are dramatically different from *good enough*. Both require differently articulated burning imperative components.

Similarly, people confuse objectives and goals. Objectives connect qualitatively with the vision. (Example: Move past competitor A to become the preferred provider in the market.) Goals must be quantitative. They must be specific, measurable, achievable, realistic, and time bound (SMART). (Example: Increase revenue by 10 percent in each product category in each of the next 3 years.)

Teams will often resort to a tagline referring to a goal (such as "10, 10, and 10!"). But as the leader, you need to make sure you keep connecting this with the objective. (Ensure a stable pipeline of new business and deliver reliably against it!) Sometimes the mission works as a headline. Sometimes the vision or priorities work. It doesn't matter. All that matters is getting everyone on the same page on direction and accountability.

Make It Happen

How do you build the individual elements—mission, vision, values, and so on—and roll them up into a burning imperative? You and your core team need to invest time into conceiving, shaping, and deciding each element and then communicating these components as a holistic, unifying burning imperative that works to focus individuals on their roles and responsibilities. It may seem daunting, but once it gets going and the team connects with the project, it develops a momentum and urgency of its own. The light clicking on for the team is one of the most exciting and memorable feelings that you and your team will ever have.

There are different ways to do this. If you don't have confidence in your team, a consultative approach tends to work best. In this case, you would draft a first-cut imperative and then get everyone else's input one at a time. This way, you never lose control of the conversation.

Tool 6.1 is designed to help you and your team reach consensus on your mission, vision, values, objectives, goals, strategies, plans, and operating cadence. The operative word is *co-creation*. You probably already have some of the components (e.g., mission, vision, objectives, strategies) in your head. They may even be down on paper. Your team members may have told you that they agree. But do they know them off the top of their heads? Do they (did they ever) really believe them? Are the components current? Inspiring? Do they create a sense of urgency and drive purposeful action? Do team members really see what they're doing as a burning imperative or just as something nice to do to pass the time? Your job as a leader is to make sure that everyone on the team can genuinely answer yes to those questions.

Bryan Smith lays out different ways of rolling out ideas: telling, selling, testing, consulting, and co-creating.[1] In most cases the best approach is co-creating. The rewards of creating together are so immense and so memorable that the process alone is the strongest antidote to silos, confusion, and indifference. You don't want the team members thinking that their mission is just a slew of buzzwords that you threw at them. Sadly, that is the destiny of many so-called burning imperatives.

The premise behind the imperative workshop is to co-create the burning imperative with your core team so that all share it. After the meeting, you should test the burning imperative by letting others in the organization consult with your core team. They may have perspectives that will lead to slight tweaks. You should be open to wording changes and some new ideas during the test, but be careful to preserve the meaning of the burning imperative that you and your team co-created. Tool 6.2 outlines remote workshop guidelines.

Do not make the mistake of attempting to let your entire organization co-create your imperative. In general, the ideal meeting size is between five and nine people. Groups of fewer than five people struggle to find enough diversity in their thinking. Groups of more than nine struggle for airtime. Additionally, if the co-creating team is too large, you're likely to end up with something that is acceptable to most and inspirational to none. By co-creating with just your core team, and perhaps one or two other key players, you can lead the team toward more inspirational ideas.

Leverage Diversity

This is also a key time to leverage diversity, foster inclusion, and ensure equality. Leverage diversity by making sure you are gaining a broad set of perspectives. Foster inclusion by making sure everyone is participating and feels comfortable sharing their thoughts. Encourage debate and spirited discussion. Ensure equality by making sure everyone has

---

[1] Peter M. Senge, Art Kleiner, Charlotte Roberts, Richard B. Ross, and Bryan J. Smith, 1994, "Building Shared Vision: How to Begin," *The Fifth Discipline Fieldbook*, Boston: Nicholas Brealey, ch. 47.

the same opportunity to contribute their ideas and take part in the delivery of the burning imperative.

Throughout the process, if someone is quiet or not participating, do not assume it's because they don't have something to say. Actively seek their engagement. Give everyone the time and space to participate. If your team that you have selected for development of the burning imperative leadership team doesn't fully represent the organization or the markets you are trying to reach, think deeply about how you can include those valuable and different perspectives in the process.

If it can't be done in the core burning imperative group, genuinely seek those perspectives when you test the burning imperative with the wider team. From your perspective, is this on target? What do you like about it? What have we missed? Are there nuances that you can share that might make this better? Is there anyone else that needs to weigh in? If you don't do this, you haven't achieved true co-creation, which is essential for the success of any burning imperative.

Done right, an imperative workshop is an intensive session with a lot of personal sharing and dialogue. Expect to learn a lot about your team members and colleagues. Expect them to learn a lot about you. It is possible that you'll end up with a burning imperative very close to what you came in with. It is more likely that you won't. Even if you do, there's power for all in the learning. As T. S. Eliot says in "Little Gidding":

> We shall not cease from exploration.
> And the end of all our exploring
> Will be to arrive where we started
> And know the place for the first time.[2]

Facilitation

In most cases, to establish an environment of co-creation, it is best if you, as the leader, do not facilitate the imperative workshop. Being a participant as opposed to the facilitator puts you in a better position to listen and understand your team's input and perspective, which will help you craft a truly co-created burning imperative. It's very hard to co-create from the front of the room. The dynamics of you sitting with the team as opposed to leading in front of the room tends

---

[2] T. S. Eliot, 1943, *Four Quartets*, New York: Harcourt Brace.

to foster a richer and more honest dialogue from the team. It's not about you. You want to emerge with a *team's* burning imperative, not the *leader's*. Don't skimp on your facilitator for this exercise. Deploy an experienced expert who is adept at guiding teams through this exercise. Facilitators play a very important role in driving a successful outcome.

Workshop Attendance and Timing

In the real world, you'll be taking over an existing team with existing priorities and existing schedules. It is unlikely that your team members will have planned to take out two days from their current work to sit around, hold hands, and sing folk songs. First point, this is real work, and the burning imperative workshop tool is focused on real business issues. It ends up being a strong team-building exercise, but as a by-product of the work. Even so, there will be some team members who are reluctant to adjust their existing schedules to accommodate this workshop, particularly if you schedule it sometime in your first 30 days (which we think is essential).

Stick with the plan. Find the date in your first 30 days that works best for most people, and then give the others the option to change their schedules or not. This approach has two advantages:

1. It keeps things moving forward in line with the 80 percent rule. Not everything is going to be perfect. Not everyone can be at every meeting. You and your team will move forward as best as you can, helping others catch up and adjusting along the way.

2. It gives you early data about different team members' attitudes and commitment. Everything communicates, and everything communicates both ways. By inviting people to a burning imperative workshop, you are sending a powerful message. Their turning it down because they have something more important to do returns a different message. How you handle overt resistance will be an important early test of your choice to assimilate, converge and evolve, or shock per the ACES model (Chapter 2).

Location

We are firm believers that the burning imperative experience is most successful when your entire team is in one room for 2 to 3 days of dedicated work. In many cases, teams fly from all corners of the globe to be together for this event. It's worth it. One of the most common comments we get from our clients after facilitating a burning imperative meeting is: "It was so valuable to all be in the room together. We need to do this more often." If you can have everyone in the room, wherever it may be its worth it. Be creative to get this done. Often clients pick locations that are centrally located to its workforce, even if they don't have an office at the location.

If possible, we encourage you to at least hold this meeting off-site. The power of being in a different place from the usual office is worth the time, money, and effort. It sends a signal that the burning imperative is an important and special meeting, pulling people away from the typical distractions of the office and clearing their minds to dive into the deep discussions required to co-create your burning imperative.

Virtual Workshops

The remote workforce is here to stay. In most companies, the days when 100 percent of the workforce are in the office are long gone. For most leaders, a hybrid model is a fact of life. It is rare to get the whole team together in one room. Maybe it's because you lead a global team, or maybe it's because current trends have changed how people in your company work, or maybe it's a younger company where a remote workforce is core to its culture, but for whatever reason, you will most likely be leading a hybrid team where some of your key stakeholders are in the office and others are not.

Hybrid meetings (where some are remote and others are in person) are tough to manage and facilitate. If you are not hypersensitive to the engagement of all, they will fail in achieving a truly co-created burning imperative. Often, those who are remote will feel like second-class citizens struggling to keep up with what's going on in the room. When a meeting is predominantly in person, those joining remotely inevitably miss some of the conversation in the room—especially when more than one person is speaking at the same time. They also miss the side conversations that happen during the meeting and during breaks.

It's physically impossible for them to get as much out of meetings as do those participating in person. Conversely, if the meeting is predominantly remote, the remote people each have their own screen and camera, while the in-person people share them. Those attending in person must fight with the other people in the room for airtime.

Depending on your organization's culture, your team's experience and level of comfort with hybrid meetings, and your facilitator's skill set, consider picking either 100 percent in person or 100 percent remote for the burning imperative meeting. If you decide to go 100 percent remote, be mindful to enforce that decision by requiring anyone in the office to join remotely and individually. Do not allow groups of people to gather in a conference room to dial in, otherwise you've defeated the purpose. However you decide to proceed, be consistent with the approach for pre–burning imperative meetings where you'll discuss prework and agendas, as well as postworkshop meetings when you're embedding milestone management, early wins, and ongoing team communications.

Remote meetings, if facilitated well, can be more *efficient*, saving on travel time and cost. One of the advantages of this is that you can spread bigger, more complex remote meetings and their breakouts over several days, allowing people to get other things done between the meeting sections and reflect on the ideas over time. To foster deeper and more meaningful interactions keep remote breakouts to four people or less whenever possible (Tool 6.2).

In-person meetings are more *effective* for humans working together or interdependently. This is because people can use all five of their senses (sight, hearing, touch, smell, taste), triggering different responses and picking up on nuances. Additionally, they can engage in side conversations during breaks, going to different layers and adjacent subjects.

Regardless of your approach, as you bring people together for a meeting, allow ample time for people to reconnect before trying to accomplish anything else. Have a bias to flexible agendas to explore and co-create versus trying to quickly converge and decide. This is one of the times where you care more about the interactions than the actual output. With patience, flexibility, and persistence, you will arrive at your outcome. First prize is to have everyone in person. Second prize is to have everyone remote. If you must, a hybrid meeting is a distant third choice. But beware, hybrid meetings are the most difficult to achieve the goal of getting your core team to invest time and work into conceiving, shaping, articulating, and communicating a unified co-created burning imperative.

Disciplined Structure

In any case, structure meetings with a clear objective, a supporting agenda, prework geared to learning, contribution, and decision-making and a stated framework for disciplined follow-up. Note the level of structure required increases with the number of people in the meeting, complexity of agenda items, and time constraints.

Prework

Prework allows you to minimize time presenting and absorbing, and maximize time learning, contributing, and deciding. Note prework is essential for introverts. It doesn't have to be long, in-depth, or complicated. It just must be enough for them to collect their own thoughts in advance. It is also helpful for those who have not felt fully included or heard in the past. From a diversity, equity, and inclusion perspective, it's often valuable to personally reach out to all team members in advance to encourage their active participation. Be aware that some may not be as comfortable or confident to contribute as others. As a leader, use this time to demonstrate the message that you will actively seek diversity of perspective and inclusion of all participants.

Finally, distribute agendas and prereading materials well in advance of the workshop and set a clear expectation that all attendees have read through the materials before the session.

Agenda

The agenda should make the overall objective for the meeting clear to attendees. For each agenda item, call out what is expected of the team—specifically, whether they should be learning, contributing or deciding.

Follow-Up

Detailed follow-up turns meetings from theoretical to truly value creating. Get the notes out quickly, partly so those who could not attend can be brought quickly up to date and weigh in with their additional thoughts (if appropriate) and mostly to kick off and coordinate value-creating actions based on the decisions the team has made.

Follow Through Consistently

Follow through and then follow through again. Pulling people together, investing the time in the effort, and then not living by it is worse than not doing it at all. A strong burning imperative is a covenant of honor.

To ensure follow-through and strong execution, you'll want to embed a milestone management process within days of completing the burning imperative workshop. This is so critical that we've dedicated the next entire chapter to the topic. Beyond that process, you must set an example by following through on your commitments and living the agreements from the burning imperative.

Gerry was a volunteer with his local life squad/ambulance service. One day he heard an accident while raking leaves in his front lawn. He ran down to the end of the street and started treating the victims, enrolling bystanders to summon the police, life squad, and help in other ways. Two of the victims walked away, and two had to be taken to the hospital. After the run to the hospital, Gerry was at the station helping to clean out the ambulance for the next call when the life squad captain walked in.

"Gerry, I noticed you were on the scene of this accident without your red life squad coat on."

Gerry explained why he had gone straight to the scene, then to the station, and then riding with the ambulance without putting his life squad coat on.

"But wearing your coat is important so people can identify you as a life squad member."

"Good point. I'll be careful the next time—Wait a minute. How did you notice I wasn't wearing my coat?"

"I drove by."

"Are you telling me you drove by the scene of a two-car accident, saw that I was the only life squad member there, and you chose to come by here and remind me to wear my coat the next time? How about stopping to help!"

It doesn't matter what words they actually used. The underlying burning imperative of every life squad, ambulance team, or first responder of any sort must be "Help people in need." This life squad captain was not living the message. You must.

If you are unclear about the differences between all these things and how they work together, stop. Go to primegenesis.com/tools for a more detailed explanation. It will be well worth your time to get familiar with these basic building blocks.

Summary and Implications

The burning imperative consists of:

Headline: The all-encapsulating phrase or tagline that defines your burning imperative

Mission: *Why* we are here and what our purpose is

Vision: Future picture—*what* we want to become, where we are going, concrete picture of success

Values: Beliefs and moral principles that guide and underpin attitudes, relationships, and behaviors

Objectives: Broadly defined, qualitative performance requirements

Goals: The quantitative measures of the objectives that define success

Strategies: Broad choices around *how* the team will achieve its objectives, including:

> **Where to play** (products/services, geographies, channels, segments)
>
> **How to win** (initiatives to deliver success)
>
> **Capabilities (**knowledge, skills, technologies, processes to deliver, strategic priorities)

Plans: Clarity on the what–who–when for programs that will bring each strategy to fruition

Operating cadence: How the team is going to implement, track, and evolve plans, together

Ownership and accountability: Clearly defined choices about who does what, who is ultimately responsible, decision-making rights, bounded authority, and accountability

The burning imperative is the pivot point for the new leader's first 100 days. Once this is established, the team moves into creating and leveraging the next wave of tactical capacity building blocks—milestone management, early wins, role sort, and evolution of leadership, practices, and culture.

For the burning imperative to drive everything everyone actually does every day, it must be truly embraced by all. Thus, you need to get it in place and shared early on—within your first 30 days at the latest. A 2- to 3-day facilitated workshop is the preferred model for making that happen.

QUESTIONS YOU SHOULD ASK YOURSELF

Have we laid the right foundation on which to build a high-performing team?

Have we done the prework with the team to have a successful workshop?

Have we sufficiently leveraged diverse perspectives to understand our context and enable co-creation?

Have we co-created a burning imperative?

Is it compelling enough to the key stakeholders?

Can the team clearly identify our focus?

Do we have the strategies and defined goals to make it real?

Does it drive purposeful action?

Is it aligned to and is it a step toward achieving our long-term purpose?

Note the most up-to-date, full, editable versions of all tools are downloadable at primegenesis.com/tools.

TOOL 6.1
Imperative Workshop

This is a 2- to 3-day, off-site workshop to drive consensus around mission, vision, values, objectives, goals, strategies, plans, and operating cadence. All members of the core team must attend. This workshop will determine the team's burning imperative.

Preparation
- In premeeting communications, set a clear destination for the meeting (mission, vision, values, objectives, goals, strategies, plans, operating cadence).

(continued)

TOOL 6.1   Imperative Workshop (continued)

- Set context—current reality—broader group's purpose.
- Send invitations, set logistics.
- Prepare to present your current best thinking (leader), or prepare to explain your role (team members).

Delivery
- Detail the destination: framework, mission, vision, values, objectives, goals, strategies, plans, operating cadence (facilitator).
- Present the current best thinking (team leader).
- Present the current subgroup roles (team members).
- Set up what matters and why.
- Review the corporate/larger group purpose (team leader).
- Revise the team's mission, vision, values, objectives, goals, strategies, plans, and operating cadence in turn by encouraging an open but focused discussion to expand ideas, group them into similar categories, select the ones that resonate most, rank them in order of importance, solicit individual drafts, collect common thoughts, and create a group draft based on input that includes the burning imperative headline (facilitator).
- Discuss how the new Imperative is different from the old situation (facilitator).
- Summarize what it will take to achieve the burning imperative (facilitator).
- Wrap up, tie the results back to the destination, and communicate the next steps (including establishing dates for defining milestone management and early wins processes).

Follow-Up
- Share with broader team for its input.
- Make refinements if required.
- Communicate the final results to all key stakeholders.

TOOL 6.2

Remote Workshop Guidelines

Session I: 90 minutes

Prep:
Pre-read: organization's mission, vision, guiding principles, strategies
+ additional prereads as appropriate

Prepare single document for breakout notes in shared workspace

[Videoconference—full group]

Welcome:
Leader's going-in perspective on mission, vision, guiding principles, priorities

Initial feedback on mission, vision, guiding principles, priorities:

—What strong? How improve?

Strategies:
Where play?

Session II: 90 minutes
Prep group's going-in perspective (potentially with SWOT)—itemized response

[Videoconference breakouts: 2–4 people + facilitator]

Strategies: How win?

Definition of success

Five big things

Competitiveness of each

(*continued*)

TOOL 6.2   Remote Workshop Guidelines (continued)

Session III: 60 minutes
Itemized response to breakout groups' ideas
> [Videoconference: full group]

Session IV: 90 minutes

Plans & Milestones:
What getting done by when by whom
> [Videoconference breakouts: 2–4 people + facilitator]

Session V: 60 minutes
Itemized response to breakout groups' ideas
> [Videoconference: full group]

Session VI: 90 minutes

Operating Principles and Procedures:
Prep group with going-in perspective
> Itemized response
> Cultural survey responses
> Discuss which cultural pieces to evolve (and how)

Close
Agreements, next steps, communication, after action review

Survey or chat = Facilitator consolidates | Iterate by e-mail |

CHAPTER 7

Drive Operational Accountability

EMBED MILESTONE MANAGEMENT BY DAY 45.

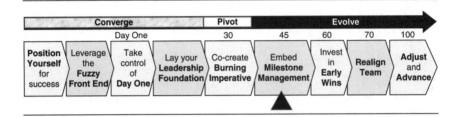

Converge					Pivot		Evolve		
Day One					30	45	60	70	100
Position Yourself for success	Leverage the Fuzzy Front End	Take control of Day One	Lay your Leadership Foundation	Co-create Burning Imperative	Embed Milestone Management		Invest in Early Wins	Realign Team	Adjust and Advance

T he real test of a high-performing team's tactical capacity lies in the formal and informal practices that are at work across team members, particularly around clarifying decision rights and information flows.[1] The real job of a high-performing team's leader is to inspire, enable, and empower others to do their absolute best, together. The most effective leaders spend more time integrating across than managing down. This is best achieved by implementing a straightforward milestone management tool that focuses on mapping and tracking who is doing what by when. High-performing team leaders exploit this milestone management tool to hold each other accountable and enable people to work together as a team!

---

[1] Gary L. Neilson, Karla L. Martin, and Elizabeth Powers, 2008, "The Secrets to Successful Strategy Execution," *Harvard Business Review*, June.

Early wins are about credibility and confidence. People have more faith in people who have delivered. You want team members to have confidence in you, in themselves, and in the plan for change. You want your boss and your colleagues to have confidence in your team's ability to deliver.

Milestones Are Checkpoints Along the Way to a Defined Goal

Recall these definitions from Chapter 5:

Objectives: Broadly defined, qualitative performance requirements

Goals: The quantitative measures of the objectives that define success

Strategies: Broad choices around how the team will achieve its objectives

Now add:

Milestones: Checkpoints along the way to achieving objectives and goals.

Capture the Milestones

Milestones are the building blocks of tactical capacity that turn a burning imperative into a manageable action plan. Your team's milestone management practice, if done right, will be a powerful team reinforcer. Milestone management is about identifying accountability, monitoring progress, and taking action to stay on track. Burning Imperative meetings tend to produce many ideas and choices on flip charts. They are all completely useless unless someone takes action to make them happen. As Steve Jobs once said, "Ideas are worth nothing unless executed. They are just a multiplier. Execution is worth millions." This chapter is about execution. In brief, to help ensure that the team delivers the desired results, in the time frame specified, you must delegate well. That involves:

- **Direction:** Clearly define objectives, goals, strategies, and desired results.

- **Resources:** Make available the human, financial, technical, and operational resources needed to deliver.

- **Bounded authority:** Empower the team to make tactical decisions within strategic guidelines and defined boundaries.

- **Accountability and consequences:** Clearly define standards of performance, time expectations, and positive and negative consequences of success and failure.

Along the way, strive for absolute clarity around:

- **Interdependencies:** Be aware of critical interdependencies that exist within the team, with other teams and projects, and with outside resources.

- **Information flows:** Know what information needs to be shared when and with whom. Ensure there is a method to share that information in a timely manner.

- **Collaboration:** Know what negotiations and joint efforts are needed to ensure alignment and adherence.

Rarely is the delivery of a milestone reliant on one person. More often than not, a milestone requires contributions from several members of the team across many functions. Despite the complexity of delivery, each milestone should be assigned one "captain" who is ultimately accountable for the delivery of that milestone. The captain is not the person required to do all the work, but rather, the key spokesperson for the communication of issues regarding the timely delivery of that milestone. The captain should be the final decision-maker, responsible for communicating across groups and ensuring needed information flows, collaboration, and delivery of the desired result. Avoid co-captains. They never work. There needs to be a single point of accountability.

Follow Through—or Don't Even Start

Sam's team put a lot of time and energy into creating a burning imperative during a 2-day workshop. The team left excited and ready to move forward. Then Sam got busy and never put the milestone management process in place. As a result, the team quickly went back to doing things the way it had been doing them before. If Sam wasn't going to follow through, why should the team?

Practices are the systems that enable people to implement the plans. They need to be coupled with systems of metrics and rewards that reinforce the desired behaviors. There is an old saying: "Show me how they are paid, and I'll tell you what they really do."

John Michael Loh, U.S. Air Force Air Combat Command, during the first Gulf War, said: "I used to believe that if it doesn't get measured, it doesn't get done. Now I say if it doesn't get measured it doesn't get approved . . . You need to manage by facts, not gut feel." As former Senator Daniel Patrick Moynihan put it, "You're entitled to your own opinions, but not your own facts."[2]

Specific performance measurements, accountabilities, and decision rights free people and teams to do their jobs without undue interference and provide the basis for nonjudgmental discussion of performance versus expectations and how to make improvements. It is essential that people know what is expected of them. When the expectations are clear, people also must have the time and resources needed to deliver against those expectations. The milestone management process is focused on clarifying decision rights and making sure that information and resources flow to where they need to go.

Milestones Enable Quicker Adjustments Along the Way

The National Aeronautics and Space Administration (NASA) and the Apollo 13 ground team provide a useful example of this. The objective of getting the astronauts back home alive after the explosion in space was compelling, but overwhelming.

It was easier to work through milestones one by one:

1. Turn the ship around so it could get back to Earth.
2. Manage the remaining power so it would last until the astronauts were back.

---

[2] Daniel Patrick Moynihan, 2008, Commencement Address, University of Pennsylvania, Philadelphia, May.

3. Fix the carbon monoxide problem so the air remained breathable.

4. Manage reentry into the atmosphere so the ship didn't burn up.

The power of milestones is that they let you know how you're doing along the way and give you the opportunity to adjust. They also give you the comfort to let your team run toward the goal without your involvement, as long as the milestones are being reached as planned.

You might evaluate your team's journey to a goal like this:

Worst case: The team misses a goal and doesn't know why.

Bad: The team misses a goal and does know why.

Okay: The team misses a milestone but adjusts to make the overall goal.

Good: The team anticipates a risk and adjusts along the way to key milestones.

Best: The team hits all its milestones on the way to delivering its goals. (In your dreams.)

Imagine that you set a goal of getting from London to Paris in 5 1/2 hours. Now imagine that you choose to drive. Imagine further that it takes you 45 minutes to get from central London to the outskirts of London. You wonder: "How's the trip going so far?"

You have no clue.

You might be on track. You might be behind schedule. But it's early in the trip, so you might think that you can make up time later if you need to. So, you're not worried.

If, on the other hand, you had set the following milestones, you would be thinking differently:

- Central London to outskirts of London: 30 minutes

- Outskirts of London to Folkestone: 70 minutes

- Channel crossing: load: 20 minutes; cross: 20 minutes; unload: 20 minutes

- Calais to Paris: 3 hours

If you had set a milestone of getting to the outskirts of London in 30 minutes and it took you 45 minutes, you would know you were behind schedule. Knowing that you were behind schedule, you could then take action on alternative options. The milestone would make you immediately aware of the need to adjust to still reach your overall goal.

You and your team are going to miss milestones. It is not necessary to hit all your milestones. What is essential is that you have put in place a mechanism to identify reasonable milestones so that you have checkpoints that allow you to anticipate and adjust along the way to reaching your destination on time.

Milestone management for your team is the same process but will require more complexity and different time horizons depending on the work:

- For multiyear efforts, you may want to set and manage annual or quarterly milestones.

- For major programs you may want to set and manage monthly milestones.

- Programs tend to be made up of projects generally managed with weekly milestones.

- Projects involve tasks, generally managed with daily milestones. The exception is in a crisis, when milestones may need to be managed even more frequently.

Manage Milestone Updates with a Seven-Step Process

Deploying a mutually supportive, team-based follow-up system helps everyone deliver results. Organizations that have deployed this process in their team meetings have seen dramatic improvements in team performance. Teams that don't, almost always fail to meet expectations. Yes, your milestone management process is that crucial. Follow these steps as well as the prep and post instructions laid out here and in Tool 7.1, and you'll be well on your way to ensuring that the team achieves its desired results on time.

Step 1: Set up. Track the action plans (what is being done, by whom, when) the team committed to during the Burning Imperative Workshop into a simple tool that is readily accessible to the team. There are several technology tools, from the simple to the robust, that can be deployed. Choose one that the team is familiar with or leverage the simple format in Tool 7.1. Decide on a date to start the milestone checkpoint meetings, ideally no more than a week after the burning imperative workshop. Agree on a frequency for the meetings, such as weekly for projects and monthly for programs so the process becomes a habit.

Step 2: Update. Require everyone to update their individual milestones and note their wins, learning and where they need help no later than 24 hours before the scheduled milestone meeting. Usually there are some logistical protocols, tracking method choices, and time frames that need to be established for submission and distribution of information before the process can begin. If you allow excuses here, the rest of the process takes a hit. Yes, it can be a pain to get it started, but once it is embedded as a team expectation and value, you'll be thankful that you endured the brief period of pain.

Step 3: Review. Require everyone to read the updates before the meeting, which enables you to take general updates and reporting off the agenda. There should be an expectation that everyone at the milestone management meeting is informed, up-to-date, and ready to focus on the most important issues. Executives often skip this step, much to the team's detriment. It seems like a straightforward process to put in place, but we've heard every reason in the book as to why it has not been implemented or why the team is not held accountable. Make no mistake, timely updates and premeeting reviews are essential elements of successful milestone management.

Step 4: Report. Use the first half of each meeting for each team member to headline wins, learnings, and areas in which the person needs help from other team members.

Resist the typical urge to work through items at this point. Require rapid, efficient, and concise reporting. It's a good idea to keep a set time limit for each individual update. (Think 3–5 minutes.) Those who tend to be long-winded might not like it, but the rest of the participants will appreciate it. A tight and controlled limit goes a long way toward making the meetings more dynamic.

Allowing discussions at this point reinforces a "first-come, first-served" mentality where the people who share later in the order tend to get squeezed for time. This is an inefficient use of time. Removing the discussion piece from the first half of the meeting gives you a chance to prioritize "where I need help from team members." This is often the most important part of the meeting. Each of these items should be captured in real time.

An alternate approach is to assume everyone has read the updates: skip the report completely and move straight into problem-solving (Step 6).

Step 5: Pause and prioritize. After everyone has had a chance to report back, take a pause. Then, prioritize a manageable number of items for discussion during the second half of the meeting.

These won't necessarily be the universally most important items because some should be worked on with a different group or subset of the team. You should make note of those items in the meeting but defer them to another meeting where the full and proper group can address them. Instead, give priority to the most important items *for this team* to work on *as a team, currently.* Try to give priority to items that are off target, in danger, or in areas where help is needed. Develop a list in descending order of priority.

Step 6: Problem-solve. Use the second part of the meeting to discuss, in order, the priority list you determined to be the team's most critical issues and opportunities.

The expectation is that the team won't get through all the items. That's okay because you're working on the most important items first— which is why you paused to prioritize. This is the time to figure out how to adjust as a team to achieve the most important goals all the while reinforcing predetermined decision rights. We outline a process for group problem-solving later in the chapter.

Step 7: Close the loop. Defer other items to the next meeting or to a separate meeting. Update the tracking reports with any changes or new directions. Communicate major shifts to those key stakeholders who need to know. Recognize team members for their efforts keeping an initiative on track.

Follow an 11-Step Process for Group Problem-Solving

Group problem-solving can be facilitated through a process that leverages preparation and working through a hypothesis (Tool 7.2):

1. Share prereading to let people think about the problem and
   potential solutions in advance. This prereading should
   include, at a minimum, the problem, current best thinking,
   context, and some potential options.

2. Start with the problem owner's current best thinking. (You'll
   need clarity around who is the problem owner and who is the
   decision-maker.)

3. Decide whether the group will discuss the problem. If yes,
   then see Step 4.

4. Answer questions for clarification (to help people understand
   context and current best thinking, not for them to comment
   on or improve the thinking—yet).

5. Highlight the most positive aspects of the current best thinking contributing to making it work.

6. Identify barriers keeping the current best thinking from
   working. (Get all the barriers on the table at the same time
   before working on any of them.)

7. Decide on the most important barrier.

8. Direct a brainstorm on the most important barrier with all
   participating, including the problem owner. Look for statements from the team members that might help remedy the
   barrier. Require statements to be in the *What you do is*
   (WYDIS) format.

9. The problem owner considers and pulls together a possible
   remedy to that barrier. Test it with the group.

10. If the tested remedy is not strong enough, continue to work
    on this barrier. If the remedy works, determine whether that
    is enough to solve the overall problem. If yes, move on to
    action steps. If not, work on the next most important barrier.

11. Action steps: Agree who will do what, by when, now that this
    problem is solved.

HOT TIP 1: Leverage the Prep

It's best if people have had the opportunity to think about the problem and potential solutions in advance, before the meeting. Encourage people to share relevant documents, analysis, and questions before the meeting. This prereading should include, at a minimum, the problem, the current best thinking, the context, and some potential options.

HOT TIP 2: Anticipate—Yellow Is Good

Anticipation is the key: At first, milestones will go from "on track" **(green)** to "oops, we missed" **(red)** with no steps in between. You'll know the process is working when people are surfacing issues they "might miss" **(yellow)** if they don't get help from others. Focus your love and attention on these "might miss" items to get the team to help. It will make people feel good about surfacing issues and will encourage them to bring future issues to the group for help.

HOT TIP 3: Banish First Come, First Served

Banish the first come, first served mentality. This milestone process is easy to deploy for disciplined people and teams. It is hard for less-disciplined people because they want to work items first come, first served. Resist that. Follow the process. You'll learn to love it. (Well, maybe not love it, but you will appreciate it. It will strengthen your team.)

HOT TIP 4: Integrate

Integrate across instead of managing down. The milestone meetings are great forums for making connections across groups. The higher you rise in the organization, the more time you'll spend integrating across and the less time you'll spend managing down. Senior managers don't like to be managed from above or have their decision rights compromised, but everyone appreciates improved information flows and interdependencies of projects and priorities across groups.

HOT TIP 5: Delegate Project Management

Let someone else project manage, directing and coordinating the mechanics of the milestone management process. This way, you can spend more time focused on people and content—inspiring, enabling, and empowering.

HOT TIP 6: Root Out the Uncommitted

Milestones uncover undisciplined and unfocused behavior. People will miss milestones. When someone misses a milestone and commits to double their efforts and make up lost ground, that's OK. When someone misses a milestone and either doesn't say anything about it or says they couldn't get to it because of other, more important priorities, it's often a sign they're not committed and do not feel accountable.

HOT TIP 7: Stay with It

As a first-time CEO, Charlie leveraged a weekly milestone management to accelerate execution of his team's growth plan after aligning on direction in his burning imperative workshop. Six years later, the team has adjusted its plans numerous times and continues to meet for 45 minutes once a week to ensure they stay on track. During this period, growth rates have doubled and the stock price has quadrupled. Charlie credits the discipline of milestone management with his team's ability to execute and adjust consistently over time.

Program and Project Management/Project Management Office

To increase clarity in the milestone management process, consider using the following definitions:

- "Enterprise-level priorities" are the most important ongoing strategic, organizational, and operational priorities and processes.

- "Programs" are the main longer-term components of those priorities, generally tracked and managed monthly.

- "Projects" are the subcomponents of programs, generally tracked and managed weekly.

- "Tasks" are the actual work that rolls up into projects, programs, and priorities. These are generally tracked and managed at least daily by frontline supervisors.

Program and projects' managers define project-specific objectives and goals, gather data, schedule tasks, and manage their program and projects' costs, budgets, and resources to deliver agreed objectives and goals.

The project management office (PMO) remit is broader: part planning, part finance, part resourcing, and part risk management, collaborating to ensure that all programs and projects are delivered with high quality and achieve their defined outcomes. This is achieved by mapping out program and project goals, defining processes, workflows, methodologies, resource constraints, and program and project scopes in collaboration with the individual program or project's manager.

In other words, the PMO is not accountable for the results of any individual program or project but is responsible for enabling all of them.

Conceive potential programs and projects in line with enterprise-level priorities.

Define programs and projects, including *team charters* to clarify the program or project teams

Purpose and Direction (Why)

- Mission, vision, priorities

- SMARTER objectives/goals: specific, measurable, achievable, realistic, time-bound, encouraging/exciting, rewarded

- Context: Information that led to objectives. Intent behind the objectives. What's going to happen after the objective is achieved.

Approach (How to think)

- Resources: human, financial, and operational resources available to the team. Other teams, groups, units working in parallel, supporting or interdependent areas.

- Guidelines: Clarify what the team can and cannot do about roles and decisions, including mandatory executional elements and enterprise-wide standards, procedures, and practices.
- Lay out the interdependencies between the team being chartered and the other teams involved.

Implementation (What to do)

- Accountability: Be clear on accountability structure—what is getting done by whom by when, update timing, completion timing, and consequences of success and failure.

Prioritize programs and projects based on return on investment—both direct (on their own) and indirect (as part of a larger program, priority, or process). This prioritization is a nontrivial effort as scope is always a function of resources (including force multipliers like methods, tools, and technologies) and time. There is a need to allocate scarce existing resources to the most important programs and projects while working to create future capabilities to expand capacity down the road.

Help assemble **resources** in line with programs and projects' scopes and move them between programs and projects as appropriate as circumstances change.

Communicate and coordinate within and across teams and with senior management.

Facilitate key meetings.

- Send out meeting notices, agendas, and requests for input.
  - Meeting agendas should include:
    - The objective of the meeting
    - Meeting timing and methodology (live, video, audio)
    - What people are being asked to do in the meeting (decide, contribute, learn)
    - Meeting attendees, their role in the meeting by agenda item (decide, contribute, learn)
    - Prereads for attendees to digest in advance to help all decide, contribute, or learn

- Facilitate, keep time, and take notes during the meeting
- Distribute notes after meeting

Enable behind the scenes to help others to do the work with methods, tools, and technologies as well as appropriate mentoring and coaching.

Manage the milestone tracking process: send out meeting notices and requests for input, following up to ensure delivery of required inputs, assembling and disseminating the inputs, facilitating milestone management meetings, issuing notes from the meetings.

Analyze data—including project budgets, finances, risks, and resource allocation—and provide appropriate reports in line with lean project management:

- **Strategize:** translate enterprise-level strategic priorities into actionable criteria
- **Collect:** collect and develop new program and project initiatives driving continuous improvement and step changes
- **Decide:** make informed decisions on new program and project initiatives and program and project conflicts
- **Execute:** implement decisions and manage programs and projects to completion

Summary and Implications

Milestones. Define them and begin tracking and managing them immediately. Compiling milestones is a waste of time if you do not have an efficient, effective, and clear process in place to track them, take action to deliver results, and adjust as necessary. Use this process to establish and reinforce expected team norms in three steps:

1. Get milestones in place.
2. Track them and manage them as a team, using an effective tool and process on a frequent and regular basis.
3. Implement a group problem-solving process.

Is everyone clear on who (roles) is doing what (goals), when (milestones), with what resources and decision rights?

Am I choosing my captains and my team members wisely?

Are we doing all we can to make sure that information and resources flow to where they need to go?

Is there a system in place to manage milestone achievement so I do not have to do it myself on an ad hoc basis?

Am I effectively using milestone management as a team-building tool?

Am I holding my team accountable to honestly update milestones on time and review the updates before the milestone meeting?

Am I certain that all my milestones are on track? If so, how can I be sure? If not, why not?

Note the most up-to-date, full, editable versions of all tools are downloadable at primegenesis.com/tools.

TOOL 7.1
Milestone Management

Use this tool to manage milestone management meetings and to follow up on progress as a team.

Milestone Management Process

1. Set up: Track what is being done, by whom, when

   Leader conducts a weekly or biweekly milestones management meeting with their team.

Prior to Milestones Management Meetings

2. Update: Each team member submits their updates.
3. Review: Each person reads and reviews updates before the meeting.

   If help is requested, relevant data, reading, analysis, and so forth are submitted in advance.

(continued)

TOOL 7.1   Milestone Management (continued)

At Milestones Management Meetings
Part One: 4 Reporting

> Each team member gives a 5-minute update in the following format: most important wins, most important learnings, areas where they need help. Reporting only. No discussion.

> Alternately, skip this and go straight to Step 6.

Part Two: 5 Pause and Prioritize

> After reporting, the leader pauses to order topics for discussion by priority.

Part Three: Problem-Solving by Priority

> Group discusses priority topics in order, spending as much time as necessary on each topic.

> The remaining topics are deferred to the next milestones management meeting or a separate meeting. Key items are updated and communicated.

Milestone Tracking

Wins:

Learning:

Where need help:

Milestones Priority Programs	When	Who	Status	Discussion/Help Needed

TOOL 7.2
Problem-Solving

1. Share **prereading** to let people think about the problem and potential solutions in advance. This prereading should include, at a minimum, the problem, the current best thinking, the context, and some potential options.

2. Start with the problem owner's current best thinking. (You'll need clarity around who is the problem owner and who is the decision-maker.)

3. Decide whether the group will discuss the problem. If yes:

4. Answer questions for clarification (to help people understand context and current best thinking, not for them to comment on or improve the thinking—yet).

5. Highlight the most positive aspects of the current best thinking contributing to making it work.

6. Identify barriers keeping the current best thinking from working. (Get all the barriers on the table at the same time before working on any of them.)

7. Decide on the most important barrier.

8. Direct a brainstorm on the most important barrier with all participating, including the problem owner. Look for statements from the team members that might help remedy the barrier. Require statements to be in the *What you do is* (WYDIS) format.

9. The problem owner considers and pulls together a possible remedy to that barrier. Test it with the group.

10. **Choice**: If the possible remedy is not strong enough, continue to work on this barrier. If the remedy works, determine whether that is enough to solve the overall problem. If yes, move on to action steps. If not, work on the next most important barrier.

11. **Action steps**: Agree who gets what done, by when, now that this problem is solved.

CHAPTER 8

Select Early Wins by Day 60 to Deliver Within 6 Months

	Converge			Pivot		Evolve		
	Day One		30	45		60	70	100
Position Yourself for success	Leverage the Fuzzy Front End	Take control of Day One	Lay your Leadership Foundation	Co-create Burning Imperative	Embed Milestone Management	Invest in Early Wins	Realign Team	Adjust and Advance

here is often a conversation about 6 months after a leader has started a new role. Someone will ask the new leader's boss how the new leader is doing. There's a good chance you have taken part in these conversations before.

"By the way, how's that new leader Rhonda doing?"

"Rhonda? She's fabulous. Love the intelligence. Love the attitude. She may be off to a slow start. But what a great hire! Really like her."

Result: Rhonda's probably on the way out, or at the very least, in real trouble. Rhonda may not find out about it for another 6–12 months, but her boss's "off to a slow start" plants a seed of doubt that could eventually lead to an unhappy ending for Rhonda.

After all, senior leaders are hired to deliver results first and foremost, and it is assumed that the required intelligence, personality, and attitude come along with the package. So, when that question is asked about your transition, you want the answer to be about specific results or early wins.

Compare the previous answer with "Rhonda? Let me tell you about all the things she's gotten done." In that scenario, Rhonda's made it. Of course, she has not done it all herself. Her team has. But Rhonda got the team focused on delivering early wins, and by doing so she gave her boss something concrete to talk about.

Early wins give the leader credibility and provide the team confidence and momentum—three exceptionally good things. For NASA and Apollo 13, fixing the oxygen problem was the early win that made the entire team believe it could succeed and gave it the confidence to deal with the rest of the challenges and the momentum to push forward despite incredible odds.

Early wins fuel team momentum and confidence. To that end, it is essential to clearly identify and jump-start potential early wins by Day 60. Once they are widely understood, the team should overinvest to deliver them by the end of your first 6 months! In general, *early wins* are not synonymous with *big wins*. They are the early, sometimes small, yet meaningful wins that start the momentum of a winning team. They are the blasting caps, not the dynamite. They are the opening singles, not the grand slam home run. They are the first successful test market, not the global expansion. They may be found by accelerating something that is already in progress instead of starting something new.

The early win prescription is relatively simple:

1. Select one or two early wins from your milestones list:
   - Choose early wins that will make a meaningful external impact.
   - Select early wins that your boss will want to talk about.
   - Pick early wins that you are sure you can deliver.
   - Choose early wins that will model important behaviors.
   - Pick early wins that would not have happened if you had not been there.
   - In many cases, the early wins start to emerge during the burning imperative meeting. Sometimes they are identified even before your Day One. Always be on the lookout for powerful early win possibilities.

2. Jump-start early wins by Day 60 and deliver by your
   sixth month:

   Early means early. Make sure that you select and jump-start early
   wins in your first 60 days that you and the team can deliver by
   the end of your sixth month. Select them early. Communicate
   them early. Deliver them early.

   Make sure that the team understands the early wins and has
   bought into delivering them on time.

   This will give your bosses the concrete results they need when
   someone asks how you are doing.

3. Overinvest resources to ensure that early wins are
   achieved on time:

   Do not skimp on your early wins. Allocate resources in a manner
   that will ensure timely delivery. Put more resources than you
   think you should need against these early opportunities so
   that your team is certain to deliver them better and faster than
   anyone thought was possible.

   Stay alert. Adjust quickly. As the leader, stay close, stay
   involved in the progress of your early wins, and react immediately if they start to fall even slightly off-track or
   behind schedule.

4. Celebrate and communicate early wins:

   As your early wins are achieved, celebrate the accomplishments
   with the entire team. This is important and should not be
   overlooked.

   Make sure that your early wins are communicated to the team
   and beyond as appropriate.

Early wins are sure to generate credibility, confidence,
momentum, and excitement. Remember the watchers? The people
who have not shown themselves to be detractors yet have also not
stood up as strong contributors. Once early wins begin, some of
the watchers will edge closer and eventually will jump in as contributors. After all, everybody wants to be part of the winning
team, right?

HOT TIP: You're Essential but the Team Gets the Win

To qualify as an early win, the result must be something that would not have been accomplished without you taking the leadership role. If it would have been accomplished without you in the role, it is not significant enough to be considered an early win. The early win should signify to the team and the other stakeholders that something has changed for the better. However, it must be seen and felt as the team's win and not your personal win alone.

Charter the Team for the Win

For the early win to create a sense of confidence and momentum in the team, the team needs to drive the win. You, as the leader, can inspire, enable, and empower by directing, supporting, and encouraging the team in the process, but it can't be your win. It must be the team's win. Therefore, your role as leader is to set the team up for success and support its efforts. The team charter and its five components are useful in doing that. They are laid out in Tool 8.1.

Summary and Implications

Early wins are about credibility, confidence, and momentum. People have more faith in people who have delivered. You want your boss to have confidence in you. You want the team to have confidence in you and in themselves. Early wins will provide that confidence.

QUESTIONS YOU SHOULD ASK YOURSELF

Have I identified an early win that will accomplish all that it needs to in terms of solidifying my leadership and giving the team confidence?

Do I have confidence in the team's strategy and tactical capacity to deliver the early win(s)?

Am I certain that I have invested enough resources to accomplish the early win(s)?

Do I have a comprehensive plan to monitor and adjust to ensure an early win victory?

What is my message when we celebrate this win—are we celebrating the win itself, the behaviors we demonstrated in order to get there, or both?

Note the most up-to-date, full, editable versions of all tools are downloadable at primegenesis.com/tools.

TOOL 8.1

Team Charter

Use this tool for getting teams off to the best start on their way to an early win.

1. Objective: What is the goal?

    a. Clearly and specifically define the early win.

    b. Use the specific, measurable, achievable, realistic, and time-bound (SMART) goal format to define specifically the early win and the required components along the way.

2. Context: Why are we doing this?

    a. Explain the intent of the early win to ensure that team members understand the collective purpose of their individual tasks.

    b. Provide sufficient information to help the team visualize the desired output. (For example, include customer requirements if they exist.)

    c. Clarify what happens next. Make sure that the team understands the follow-on actions to ensure that momentum is sustained after the win is delivered.

3. Resources: What help do we need?

    a. Ensure that the team has and can access all the human, financial, and operational resources needed to deliver the objective. (Remember, for an early win, you're going to overinvest in resources to ensure delivery.)

    b. Clarify what other teams, groups, and units are involved and what their roles are.

    c. Allocate resources in a timely manner to ensure delivery.

    d. Decide what essential data is needed to measure results.

(continued)

TOOL 8.1   Team Charter (continued)

---

   e. Provide frequent and easy access to required data.

   f. Let the team know you are available to help as they encounter obstacles along the way.

   g. Guidelines: How are we empowered to do this?

   h. Clarify what the team can and cannot do with regard to roles and decisions.

   i. Lay out the interdependencies between the team being chartered and the other teams involved.

4. Accountability: How will we track and monitor?

   a. Clarify what is going to get done by when by whom and how the team and you are going to track milestones so that you can know about risks in advance and can intervene well before milestones are missed.

   b. Clarify command, communication, and support arrangements so that all know how they are going to work together.

   c. Schedule regular updates.

   d. Monitor and adjust along the way to achieve that purpose while minimizing unintended consequences.

   e. Know the signs when course corrections or reevaluations are necessary.

CHAPTER 9

Build a High-Performing Team

Realign, Acquire, Enable, and Mentor by Day 70.

Converge				Pivot		Evolve		
		Day One		30	45	60	70	100
Position Yourself for success	Leverage the **Fuzzy Front End**	Take control of **Day One**	Lay your **Leadership Foundation**	Co-create **Burning Imperative**	Embed **Milestone Management**	Invest in **Early Wins**	**Realign Team**	**Adjust and Advance**

Of all the tools in your toolbox, building a high-performing team is one of the most powerful. It is also the most explosive. As you seek to evolve (or shock!) the culture, decisions around realigning, acquiring, enabling, and mentoring team members are the most public and impactful ones you will make.

Often, team members of a culture or organization that is beginning to evolve will watch and wait to see whether there are any consequences for not evolving with the new culture. They will pay particular attention to the team members who say things like, "All that meeting and report stuff is fine, but if it means I have to change what I do, forget it!" The moment somebody is terminated or moved or promoted, those who have been resisting the change often develop a completely different view of things. There is no single way to impact culture more quickly than changes to the organization.

Everybody on the team feels it when personnel moves are made. Everyone will have an opinion (usually strong) on the moves and how they affect them. Team member moves spark emotions, fears, and egos, so you need to be thoughtful about who, what, and especially when you move people. Recognize that moving people should be seen as your most potent communication tool: This person means business and means it now!

As a leader, you can help your team and the people you're working with see their roles in a more comprehensive light if you try to link them directly to their career development. Many people are not in the right role for the team's mission or even for their own professional development. Moving roles is often as much about doing what is right for the individual as it is for the team. If you can develop the leadership skill of communicating with people effectively about roles and careers, you will be investing not only in the success of your 100 days but also in your own long-term success as a leader.

The Structure and Roles Can Be the Cause of Problems

Keep in mind that you will inherit not only a team but also a structure and set of roles that might range from tightly defined to loosely implied. Don't make the mistake of assuming that the structure and roles are properly defined for what the group is trying to achieve. Often, they are years old and were created for a mission and a set of goals that no longer exist. Take a step to eliminate ambiguity and clarify roles and responsibilities that precisely match the team's burning imperative. Therefore, you may want to wait until Day 70—by then, you have established your burning imperative (confirming the core focus of the business and providing strategic and operating context for structure and roles) and observed team members in action (providing context for matching individuals to roles).

Sometimes a team member is well suited for 90 percent of what's required in the role but is seen as underperforming because they struggle with the 10 percent of the role that is not a match for him or her. Those mismatch elements of a role are *role outliers*. Role outliers are relative to the individual, not the role itself. They might make sense as a part of a greater role, but not when assigned to a particular individual as part of that role.

Sometimes role outliers can be revealed with one simple question: What's the least favorite part of your job? Listen to the answer, probe for more information, and you'll eventually uncover the obvious culprits. Find these and root them out. Assign those role outliers to others on the team who may be better suited to deliver against the requirement. Slight changes in role can have a dramatic impact on performance, levels of engagement, and satisfaction. Don't be afraid to be creative and avant-garde when redefining roles.

Sometimes the talent you need to deliver on your burning imperative does not sufficiently exist on the team. Or as the team structure or roles are redefined there may be new roles that emerge that are best filled from looking outside the team or outside the organization. If you must acquire additional talent with greater or different strengths, move quickly but choose wisely. New additions to the team (and their skill sets) should send clear signals that strongly reinforce the team's burning imperative and its evolving culture.

When Barry took over as chief executive officer of a marketing services company in London, he identified a need to dramatically improve the company's customer service capability. The company's ability to serve its customers had not kept up with the pace of innovation. This issue was identified and accepted as a priority by the team during the burning imperative workshop.

Responsibility for customer service sat with the vice president of sales, and despite positive intentions he was unable to give the group the attention it required as its mission evolved. The customer service team was focused on *reacting* to queries, *not proactively* solving problems and ensuring strong usage and satisfaction. As the business evolved, fixes required input from others outside the customer service team. Cross-functional collaboration was required but the customer service team still needed to lead the way.

Given the urgency for better customer service, Barry carved the group out of sales and had them temporarily report directly to him. Immediately the team co-created enhanced customer service requirements and then restructured individual roles to ensure that the entire team was focused on delivering a far more proactive customer experience. Armed with new service objectives and enhanced role clarity, Barry appointed a committed team member to the new role of director of customer experience to lead the charge.

With a new focus on customer service objectives, greatly increased role clarity, and a leader focused on implementing, the team quickly made great strides in customer service and satisfaction. In addition, free from the burden of managing customer service, the sales leader was able to focus more of his time on developing a stronger sales organization, and sales began to increase.

A Framework for Planning

When it comes to sorting people and roles on your team, you need to work with a short-term and a long-term framework. Initially, determine whether any short-term moves should be made by Day 70. Then, in the longer term, to develop your team. This chapter deals with the shorter time frame. We'll go into more depth on some of the longer-term aspects in Chapter 10.

Align Everything Around Your Core Focus and Burning Imperative

Start by defining the structure and set of roles that you need to realize your mission, execute your strategy, and deliver on your goals. The mission determines the makeup of the ideal organization over the long run. The resulting strategies and plans help determine what roles are required to do the things that need to be done daily to achieve the goals. This gives you a map of the roles you need to have and the roles you may need to eliminate. This is also the time to root out the role outliers.

As discussed in Chapter 6, all organizations design, produce, sell, deliver, and service. The core focus of your business will indicate which one of those actions is your primary function. Once this has been identified, your first job is to align all functions to support it in terms of organization and operations (Figure 9.1).

Implement ADEPT Talent Management

Once you've determined your core focus and have aligned your purpose, organizational structure, operations approach, culture, and leadership focus to that core and your burning imperative, you'll now want to think in terms of **A**cquiring, **D**eveloping, **E**ncouraging, **P**lanning, and **T**ransitioning (ADEPT) talent to accelerate team development. The headlines are in Table 9.1.

FIGURE 9.1   Core Focus

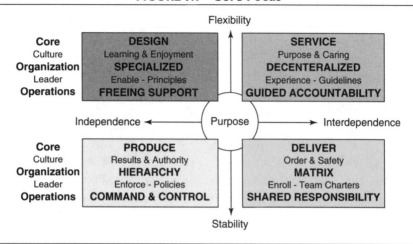

Keep your core focus in mind as you acquire, develop, encourage, plan, and transition people.

Table 9.1
ADEPT Framework for Talent Management

Acquire	Scope roles. Precision, depth, and clarity are essential.
	Identify prospects.
	Recruit and select the right people with the right talent for the right roles.
	Attract those people.
	Onboard them so that they can deliver better results faster.
Develop	Assess performance drivers.
	Develop skills, knowledge, experience, and craft for current and future roles.
Encourage	Provide clear direction, objectives, measures, and so on.
	Support with the resources, authority, and time required for success.
	Reinforce desired behaviors with recognition and rewards.
Plan	Monitor people's performance over time.
	Assess their situation and potential.
	Plan future capability development, succession, and for contingencies.
Transition	Migrate people to different roles to fit their needs/life stage and company needs.

Role Requirements

With a picture of ideal structure and roles in hand, you can now determine which roles will have the greatest impact on delivering against your mission, strategies, and goals. The roles responsible for these tasks are the critical ones. The other roles encompass tasks that can be done merely well enough. This is where strategy and people overlap. At this point, determine which roles need to be best in class and invested in and which roles can be maintained or outsourced.

The airline industry has historically lost buckets of money over the long term, yet Southwest makes money every year. Part of why it does is that it has figured out which are its critical roles. Southwest overinvests in maintenance roles so it can turn its planes around faster. It overinvests in training its flight attendants so passengers' in-air experience is fun. Conversely, it underinvests in food service and on-the-ground waiting spaces.

Identify what roles will enable you to:

- Win with capabilities that are predominant, superior, or strong, compared with others
- Play not to lose by being above average or good enough
- Choose to outsource, ally with others, or not do at all

Right People in the Right Role

Now that you have defined the right structure and set of roles, and determined the requirements for success in those roles, it is time to see whether you've got the right people in the right roles (current) and who should be placed in new roles. It's unlikely that you'll acquire a team that is perfectly set up to deliver against your burning imperative. If you're lucky, with a couple of small tweaks you'll be on your way to a world-class team. However, if there is a significant need for change, you may need to do a major overhaul. If so, be prepared for a lot of work and a lot of disruption. The earlier you make that assessment, the better. Don't make the mistake of delaying or avoiding the people changes that need to be made while hoping that some magical transformation will occur. It won't.

For some reason, it is human nature to put off such decisions. Yet the number one regret experienced senior leaders express is not moving fast enough on people. Have a strong bias for figuring the right role sort out as early as possible and making the moves quickly. Getting the right people in the right roles with the right support is a fundamental, essential building block of a high-performing team. Without the right people in the right roles, there is no team.

Getting the right people in the right roles is guided by the team's mission, vision, and values as well as by individuals' strengths. Strengths are necessary for success. But they are not sufficient. People must want to do well, and they must fit in. It is helpful to think in terms of strengths, motivation, and fit.

Strengths

Match the right people with the right roles. In their book *Now, Discover Your Strengths,* Marcus Buckingham and Don Clifton's core premise is that people do better when they capitalize on their own individual strengths, which comprise talent, knowledge, and skills. According to Gallup, "A strength is the ability to consistently provide near-perfect performance in a specific activity. The key to building a strength is to identify your dominant talents, then complement them by acquiring knowledge and skills pertinent to the activity." Use a tool such as Gallup's Clifton Strengths Assessment to help you better match talent to roles and as a valuable aid in career development for your team.[1]

It's useful to add hard-won experience to this base model because people learn from their failures and mistakes—hence "hard-won." In some rare cases, people take these strengths to craft-level based on their artistic caring and sensibilities. This suggests a more complete view of strengths includes innate talent, learned knowledge, practiced skills, *plus* hard-won experience and apprenticed craft.

Motivation

If you understand your people's values, your people's goals, and how they see what they are currently doing considering those goals, you have a terrific advantage in helping them find or live up to the right role for themselves and for the organization. Look at recent performance reviews, go back to your journaling during your early days of onboarding (when you were developing your first impressions), and reflect on the observations you have made during your first weeks on the job.

---

[1] Marcus Buckingham and Donald Clifton, 2001, *Now, Discover Your Strengths,* New York: Free Press.

Fit

Fit is determined by how well an individual's cultural preferences match with the organization's culture. Take a hard look at attitudinal perspective, values, and biases.

Perspective is an attitude born out of how people have been trained to view and solve business problems. It is the accumulation of people's business experience as manifested in their mental models. People with a classic sales perspective may feel that they can sell any product to customers. Conversely, people with a more marketing perspective may feel the organization should modify its products and services to meet customers' needs. It's not that one perspective is better than the other, just that they are different.

It is rare for all of any individual's values to match all of the organization's values. However, it is important for most of the core values to match and for none of them to be in direct conflict with each other.

Different people behave at work in different ways. Some roles may require people with a greater sense of urgency. Some roles require people who think things through thoroughly before jumping in. If someone who tends to get a later start on the day is assigned the role of generating overnight sales reports for the group before everyone else comes in, it would force the person to work in opposition to a natural bias and would most likely be a recipe for failure (and inaccurate reports).

When Things *Aren't* Working, Don't Wait

We've run over 50 CEO boot camps over the past 2 decades, each with 8–12 CEOs and other experts in the room. The regret about not moving fast enough on people in the wrong roles kept coming up.

Couple that with the number one thing high performers want, which is for someone to get the deadwood or other obstacles out of their way, and it's no surprise that when leaders finally do move on people in the wrong roles, they are met with others asking, "What took you so long?" And as one CEO put it, he knew some of them were thinking, "We were beginning to doubt your judgment."

Some leaders think they're being nice by waiting. They're not. At some level, people in the wrong roles know they're in the wrong roles. The sooner you can move them into the right role (either in your organization or elsewhere), the better for all involved.

How Fast Should You Move on the Team?

In general, have your plan in place to sort roles and make people moves at the end of 70 days or 10 weeks. There will be times when you need to move much faster and times when it will take you longer to implement the plan, but the seventieth day is a good target time frame to have it all figured out.

There is a risk in moving too fast. The risk is that you'll make poor decisions and come across as too impulsive. By the seventieth day, you will have had a chance to see people in the Burning Imperative workshop, in the milestone management process, and for some of them, in the pursuit to deliver on an early win. By Day 70, you should have enough information to make those crucial decisions.

There's a larger risk in moving too slowly. At about 100 days, you own the team. Once you own the team, the problem children become your problem children. You can't blame the team's failings or unresolved issues on your predecessor anymore. Also, the other team members know who the weak links are, and they might have known since before you took the helm. They will want you to make the tough moves. The number one thing high performers want is for management to act on low performers so the whole group can achieve more. If you move too slowly, the other team members will wonder what took you so long.

To be clear, you may not be able to implement your decisions all at once. You may need to put in place transition plans that support weaker team members or keep strong team members in the wrong roles during the time it takes to get their replacements on board and up to speed. It's not that you should make all your moves in your first 70 days, no matter what. But you should have the plan in place and begin making moves at an intentional pace and do so with a bias toward making the moves sooner rather than later.

HOT TIP

Have a bias to move faster on your team than you think you should. The risks of moving too fast are nothing compared with the multiplier effect of leaving people in the wrong place too long.

Map Performance and Role

Putting the right people in the right roles is a key driver of success. The heart of Tool 9.1 is a grid that matches people with roles. The grid is based on two dimensions: performance and role match. Mapping people on this grid helps inform decisions about which people are in the right roles and which are in the wrong roles, so you can support some and move others. This is a simple but highly effective tool for thinking about a complex subject.

The performance measure is drawn from an individual's last or current review/assessment in his or her current role. It is driven by results versus goals and supplemented with recently observed performance, behaviors, and communication.

The role match measure is a correlation of the strengths, motivations, and fit required for the role compared with the strengths, motivations, and fit of the person filling that role. The role's strengths, motivations, and fit should be drawn from position descriptions. The individual's strengths, motivations, and fit could be drawn from their latest review, Gallup's Clifton Strengths, or another assessment questionnaire or tool.

Keep in mind that some people may be in the wrong role precisely because they have outgrown it and are ready for a promotion. If you leave these people in their roles, you'll face a growing risk for decreased motivation or, worse yet, unwanted resignations. If there is an indication that an individual is struggling to make up for a mismatch between personal strengths and those required for the job, it is also a sure sign of a mismatch. Evolving is the appropriate action for these people. In either situation, the value of having a plan to move each candidate to a more appropriate role is clear. Delay those moves and you'll find yourself and your team in trouble.

When managing talent, most organizations fail to differentiate. Treating everyone the same produces an undermotivated, uninspired, and less-evolved team. Each team member should have a highly personalized talent development plan.

Start by sorting based on performance (underperforming, effective, or outstanding) and whether they are in the right roles. Tool 9.1 will be helpful with your analysis.

As a general and starting guideline, try to limit your outstanding ratings, regardless of role fit, to just 10–15 percent of the team. Expect to find most people effective and in the right role. Support them as a top priority. Then treat your other people differently, cherishing outstanding performers in the right roles and doing what it takes to help others improve their performance or circumstances.[2]

Strong Performers and the *Three Goods*

Invest in your strong performers first. Way too many leaders get sucked into spending so much time dealing with underperformers that they don't pay enough attention to the people in the right roles performing particularly well until those people walk in to announce they're leaving.

Instead, treat your strong performers so "good" all along the way that they will not ever be open to the conversation about possibly leaving. Remember, this is three goods:

- *Good for others:* Inspire your strong performers with the *good for others* part of your mission or purpose.

- *Good at it:* Do what it takes to remove any barriers that hinder your strong performers' ability to do more of what they are good at.

- *Good for me:* Ensure your strong performers receive the recognition and rewards they deserve. As your strong performers' knowledge, skills, and accomplishments grow, make sure the person recognizing and rewarding their new market worth is you.[3]

Position Profiles and Potential

Mapping performance and role appropriateness facilitates an urgent identification of who is in the right role and who is in the wrong role now. It is important not to confuse *role match* with *potential* because there is a significant difference between the two. Role match focuses on the current position. What's the likelihood of their performing well in their current position? Potential focuses on growth, development, and future promotions. What is required to help people move up the ladder? What is the appropriate timeline for those promotions?

---

[2] George Bradt, 2017, "The Only Six Variable Approaches to Talent Management: Invest, Support, Cherish, Move Up, Over or Out," *Forbes*, June 14.
[3] George Bradt, 2015, "Why You Should Never Make or Take Counter Offers," *Forbes*, November 18.

Position profiles are formalized ways to set the foundations for achievement within an organization at any given role. Every organization has its own way of doing position profiles. When done well, these can be used when acquiring, evaluating, mentoring, developing, and promoting talent. The better position profiles include the key elements of the mission, vision, strengths, motivation, and fit relative to the position. Some benchmarks to consider in each of these areas are detailed in the next section.

Developing Future Leaders

When people see or hear *leader*, they generally think of interpersonal leaders inspiring and enabling teams. Although those interpersonal leaders are of critical import, many organizations need artistic leaders and scientific leaders as well. The common characteristic of all leaders is that they inspire others to become better than they would on their own. Each of the three types of leaders inspire others in different ways (Table 7.2):

Artistic leaders inspire by influencing feelings. They help us take new approaches to how we see, hear, taste, smell, and touch things. You can find these leaders creating new designs, new art, and the like. These people generally have no interest in ruling or guiding. They are all about changing perceptions.

Scientific leaders guide *and* inspire by influencing knowledge with their thinking and ideas. You can find them creating new technologies, doing research and writing, teaching, and the like. Their ideas tend to be well thought through, supported by data and analysis, and logical. These people develop structure and frameworks that help others solve problems.

Interpersonal leaders can be found ruling, guiding, and inspiring at the head of their interpersonal cohort, whether it's a team, organization, or political entity. They come in all shapes and sizes, and influence actions in different ways. The common dimension across interpersonal leaders is that they are leading other people.

Table 9.2
Artistic, Scientific, and Interpersonal Leadership Characteristics

	Interpersonal	Scientific	Artistic
Where to play?	Context	Problems	Media
What matters/why?	Cause	Solutions	Perceptions
How to win?	Rally team	Better thinking	New approach
How to connect?	Hearts	Minds	Souls
What impact?	Actions	Knowledge	Feelings

Ask yourself what type of leader does your team need the most, in each role? Is there a certain type of leader that is needed but not yet on the team? Evaluate all team members on their leadership potential and their natural type, and you'll start to find valuable clues on how to best develop them for continued success. One hallmark of the strongest leaders is their ability to develop other leaders along the way. Develop as many as you can, and when you do, you'll leave a legacy on your organization that will deliver consistent growth and inspire many lives.

Summary and Implications

Start by defining the right structure and roles to execute on your mission. Be specific about talent, knowledge, skill, and experience requirements for success in each key role, and then match them with the right people.

Make your organization stronger by acquiring, developing, encouraging, planning, and transitioning talent:

Acquire: Recruit, attract, and onboard the right people with the right talent.

Develop: Assess and build skills, knowledge, experience, and craft.

Encourage: Direct, support, recognize, and reward.

Plan: Monitor, assess, and plan career moves over time.

Transition: Migrate to different roles as appropriate.

Pay attention to differences. The world needs three types of leaders: scientific leaders who influence knowledge, artistic leaders who influence feelings, and interpersonal leaders who influence actions. These three are not always mutually exclusive. Jump-start your team by getting the right people in the right roles with the right support to build the team.

Some of your most painful choices are going to be in this area. Trying to please everybody will lead to pleasing nobody. Choosing to act on people who are in the wrong roles now or will soon be in the wrong roles is generally not the most enjoyable part of leadership. But it is an essential part.

QUESTIONS YOU SHOULD ASK YOURSELF

Am I moving at the right speed to get the right people in the right roles?

Have I defined the right organizational structure and set of roles?

Am I making the tough choices on people as soon as I have identified a mismatch?

Am I considering the right balance of leadership skills and styles on my leadership team?

Do I have adequate development plans in place?

Do I have appropriate backup and contingency plans?

Am I creating an environment where future leaders are encouraged to emerge and develop?

Note the most up-to-date, full, editable versions of all tools are downloadable at primegenesis.com/tools.

TOOL 9.1

Role Sort

	Underperforming 15–20%	Effective 65–70%	Outstanding 10–15%
In right role	**Invest** (to improve performance)	**Support** (in current role)	**Cherish** (with extra attention)
In wrong role	**Move Out** (quickly with compassion and respect)	**Move Over** (quickly with an onboarding plan)	**Move Up** (with an onboarding plan and mentorship)

Underperforming in Right Role: Invest

Do what it takes to define their roles, fix their management, give them the training or resources they need, and they will perform.

Effective in Right Role: Support

Invest appropriately to support in current roles, helping them continue to grow, perform, and be happy.

Outstanding in Right Role: Cherish

Overinvest to help them grow, perform, and be happy in their current roles.

Underperforming in Wrong Role: Move Out

Treat with respect and compassion and move them out with a minimum of discretionary investment.

Effective in Wrong Role: Move Over

Find them and move them to the right role before they burn out or quit.

Outstanding in Wrong Role: Move Up

Promote them before somebody hires them away. Move them up sooner than you're comfortable and with more support to succeed in their new roles.

TOOL 9.2
Recruiting Brief

Recruit for job title, department, compensation grade, start date:

Mission/Responsibilities

Why does this position exist?

What are the objectives, goals, and desired outcomes?

What is the desired impact on the rest of the organization?

What are the specific responsibilities of the role?

(continued)

TOOL 9.2   Recruiting Brief (continued)

What organizational relationships and interdependencies are important?

What is the vision (picture of success) for the role?

Strengths

What talents are required? (Innate)

What knowledge is required? (Learned: education, training, experience, qualifications)

What skills are required? (Practiced: technical, interpersonal, business)

What experience is required? (Hard-won)

What level of craft is required? (Artistic caring and sensibilities)

Motivation

How do the activities of the role fit with the person's likes/dislikes/ideal job criteria?

How will the person progress toward the desired long-term goal?

Fit

What are the desired behaviors, relationships, attitudes, values, environmental preferences for the role?

What are the characteristics of the company's work style?

What are the characteristics of the group's work style?

What are the characteristics of the supervisor's work style?

How well does the candidate fit with each of these characteristics?

Adjust and Advance Your Own Leadership, People, Practices, and Culture by Day 100

Converge						Pivot		Evolve		
Day One					30		45	60	70	100
Position Yourself for success	Leverage the Fuzzy Front End	Take control of Day One	Lay your Leadership Foundation	Co-create Burning Imperative	Embed Milestone Management		Invest in Early Wins	Realign Team		Adjust and Advance

You have reached the 100-day mark. You put a plan in place, leveraged your fuzzy front end to learn quickly, refined your plan, and developed solid relationships with all of your key stakeholders. You engaged the culture and made a strong early impression by delivering a clear message to your new audiences (up, down, and across). Your team is energized by its co-created burning imperative. You have established a milestone management process to drive accountability and are beginning to deliver early wins. You've assessed your team and begun to realign it around the future needs of the business.

So, what's next? Keep adjusting. Keep advancing. You'll want to evolve in four key areas:

1. **Your Leadership:** The 100-day mark is a good moment to gain feedback on your own leadership. You should take a moment and determine what you should keep, stop, and start doing to be even more effective with your direct report team and the organization as a whole.

2. **People:** Decide how you are going to evolve your people and related processes in line with changing circumstances.

3. **Practices: Milestone Management, Long-Term Planning, and Program Management:** Assess whether you've been measuring the right things and have built adequate practices to develop and implement your plans.

4. **Culture:** Finally, after 100 days, your insights on the culture are sharper than when you started. You are also clearer about where you want to evolve the culture. Zero in on the biggest gaps and implement a plan to create and maintain the winning culture that will become your greatest competitive advantage.

Adjust and Advance Your Leadership

Take a three-step approach to adjusting and advancing your leadership.

Step 1: **Assess your effectiveness as a leader**, defining areas you need to adjust to be more effective.

Refer to whatever documents you have available—your original 100-day plan, your milestone management document, your culture-change tracking forms, your progress on increasing diversity, or your recent financial results—and assess how you have performed versus the goals that you (and your board and your boss) set. Rate yourself green if you are on track, yellow if you are at risk (yet have a solid plan to get back on track), and red if you will miss (and do not have a solid plan to get back on track). Ask your boss to do the same to identify disconnects in perceptions or expectations.

Next, collect 360-degree feedback on your performance from your critical stakeholders up, across, and down. (Answer the same questions yourself so you can compare your own thoughts with that of others.) Doing this will help you (1) see how others feel, (2) highlight disconnects between how you and others see you, and (3) model the behavior of seeking and considering personal input from others. Questions:

- What are you doing that is particularly effective that you should *keep* doing?

- What are you doing that gets in the way of your effectiveness that you should *stop* doing?

- What else could you do to be even more effective that you should *start* doing?

Step 2: **Prepare a leadership development plan** that specifies not only *what* to focus on to drive results but also *how* you need to communicate and lead the members of your team to drive engagement.

Informed by the outputs from the self-assessment and 360-degree feedback, build your development plan. Define key deliverables across strategic, operational, and organizational matters and key leadership habits you need to strengthen to become even more effective.

Step 3: **Identify support partners** to help you refine your plan and stay on track. Start by leveraging your boss to ensure you stay on track with priorities. Establish a rolling agenda with the right balance of fixed and changeable items and a regular communication cadence. If one of your needs is for greater organizational planning, utilize your assistant or chief of staff to ensure your time is being managed toward the key items. If its behavioral coaching you need, enroll a trusted mentor or former boss, a board member, your human resources (HR) partner, an external coach, or a consultant.

In any case, find the support to help you turn your desire into action and your action into habits. You will evolve and become an even better leader for the effort.

Develop Your Team

The 100-day mark is a good time to dial up your focus on developing your people as individuals, and your team as a whole, ensuring that they are positioned for longer-term success.

Set in motion a process to align the longer-term organizational development plans with the longer-term (3-plus years) strategic plan. Consider these four components:

1. **Future capability development planning** starts with the long-term strategy and then looks at what human capabilities you're going to need over time to implement that long-term plan. Compare this future-state organizational plan with your current-state organization to identify where the gaps exist between the two. Generally, you'll plan to close those gaps with a combination of:

   - Developing your current people by enhancing their innate talent with learned knowledge, practiced skills, assignments to give them hard-won experience and a chance to flex their skills and talents, and apprenticed craft-level artistic caring and sensibilities

   - Acquiring people with new talents and developing them over time

   - Acquiring people requiring less development closer to the time of need

   - Acquiring people ready to go at the time of need

2. **Succession planning** starts with the people you have in place in key roles and lays out who can take their places over time. Some of those potential successors may require development.

3. **Contingency planning** evaluates who can jump in and fill a position if one of your leaders is unable to fulfill the role for some reason. Some of these seat fillers may be permanent. Some may be on interim assignments. Some may be outsiders brought in for a short period.

4. **Performance management and talent reviews** monitor the progress of individual development plans and help people maximize their potential by giving the appropriate people the training to build their knowledge, projects where they can practice and build skills, and assignments to gather experience.

Schedule these four processes to be done on an annual basis.

Enhance Practices: Milestone Management, Program Management, and Long-Term Planning

Milestone Management

By now, you should be well on your way to tracking milestones to keep the team focused on the most important deliverables, as a team. You should be doing this monthly, unless milestones are falling off target, in which case you should increase the frequency until the milestones are back on track.

At this point you'll want to pause to evaluate your tracking process. Is it working as planned? Are we tracking the right milestones? Are our meetings efficient and focusing on the most important issues? Analyze and adjust as necessary.

Long-Term Planning

You'll also want to ensure that you have the proper balance between long-term thinking and short-term execution. Consider blending in longer term issues (talent reviews, strategic planning and reviews, future capability, succession and contingency planning, operational reviews) on a quarterly meeting schedule to ensure that each is addressed at last once annually.

The idea is to have a meeting every month with time added once each quarter to deal with longer-term issues. It is a cycle with each piece feeding into the next. Use the calendar in Table 10.1 as a starting point, and then adjust it to meet your organizational needs without dropping any key pieces.

Table 10.1
Prototypical Quarterly Meeting Flow

Monthly	Milestone Update and Adjustments
Middle month each quarter:	Business Review and Adjustments plus a deep dive on a special topic
	Special Topics:
	Q1: Talent Reviews
	Q2: Strategic Review and Planning
	Q3: Future Capability, Succession and Contingency Planning
	Q4: Operational Review and Planning
	Leverage Tool 10.1 for Business Reviews.

Program Management

If you haven't already, now is the time to consider a project/program management capability. As a new leader, whether you are replacing an incumbent in an existing role or stepping into a new one created by a merger, acquisition, or reorganization, you are likely being asked to transform your organization and take performance to a higher level in a period that is much shorter than you may be accustomed to (particularly if you are operating in a private equity–owned or venture capital–owned environment).

As a result, it is likely there will be several new projects being introduced to the team. They might be projects to drive innovation, sales effectiveness, expense reduction, or operational excellence; benchmark human capital needs; upgrade systems; upgrade teams; or identify alliance partners and merger and acquisition targets.

By Day 100, you will have a feel for the organization's ability to absorb the amount of change you wish to drive and the number of new projects you can successful implement concurrently. If the number of initiatives is overwhelming, and it probably will be, you can increase team capacity by introducing a program management capability.

Program management is the process of managing several related projects, with the intention of improving the organization's performance. The benefit of a program management skill set on the team is the ability to look across multiple projects for dependencies, bottlenecks, resourcing issues, and time conflicts. A strong program manager can identify challenges, bring choices into the light, and enable decision-making by the team. For some new teams, managing one or two new projects in addition to daily responsibilities is plenty complex. Imagine when multiple projects, not to mention large ones like acquisitions, are introduced. Chaos ensues!

You may find program management skill sets already reside in your organization. The likely places to look are information technology, operations, finance, strategy, and product development. If you do not have the requisite skills in-house, consider hiring full- or part-time project and program management experts to help you manage the numerous initiatives to their desired outcomes. See Tool 10.3.

Evolve Your Culture

Now that you are 100 days into your new role, it is a good time to evolve the organization even more assertively to your target culture.

As described in the executive summary, think about the new leader's role in building culture as a five-phase process:

1. Identify your cultural preferences (Prepare yourself for success).
    At this stage you evaluated the degree of cultural fit from your perspective, before accepting and starting the job.

2. Observe the organization's defined and undefined cultural identity (Leverage your fuzzy front end).
    At this stage you purposefully gathered information to prepare yourself for the culture you were about to enter.

3. Craft your own cultural engagement plan (before Day One).
    At this stage:

    - You determined your level of assertiveness in entering the organization (shock, assimilate, or converge and evolve) based on your assessment of the organizational need for change versus its readiness for change.

    - You identified your stakeholders as detractors, supporters, or watchers to help focus your relationship-building efforts.

    - You built and refined your going-in messaging, reflecting the platform for change and call to action for the team.

4. Begin to influence and drive the culture during your first 100 days.

At this stage:

- You sent messages early and often signifying what was important to you (your values) by what you said and where and with whom you spent time.

- You co-created a burning imperative that was a huge step in defining the culture, by gaining alignment on mission, vision, values, strategies, actions, and operating cadence.

- You established a milestone management tool and pushed for early wins to set a cultural tone.

- You made decisions on people and structure and communicated them in a way to support changing the culture toward your vision.

5. Evolve the culture after Day 100.

Three-Part Approach

First, make sure you and your leadership team are aligned on the specific values and behaviors you are attempting to embed into the culture.

Second, work with your leadership team to evaluate where you are as an organization against the dimensions of a culture: behaviors, relationships, attitudes, values, and the environment (BRAVE). Identify where you believe you need to focus as a team to move closer to the desired state.

Third, now that you and your leadership team are aligned on BRAVE, and clear about where you need to evolve across those components, begin to make changes in business processes that reflect where you are heading. Reinforce the changes by ensuring your core people processes work for you to embed the desired culture, over time.

Performance Feedback and Reward and Recognition

Provide feedback not only on measurable results but also on demonstrated behaviors in line with the target culture. Do this in the moment of the behavior as frequently as possible.

Publicly recognize those who've not only delivered concrete results but also demonstrated desired behaviors.

Internal Communication

An active internal communications program is the lifeblood of a cultural evolution. First, get your messages clear on what you wish to reinforce about the culture you are driving. If people need to work more closely as a team to solve customer problems, institute a Lunch & Learn or similar program to share information and get on the same page. Or encourage leadership team members to invite peers to their staff meeting to share news from their departments. If you are trying to evolve the team and the culture to a more aggressive posture in the market, celebrate examples where team members were assertive, took a risk, and won the business.

The ideas will flow; just be sure you do map your messages to your audiences and have a continuous and multimedia approach to communicating culture.

NOTE CULTURE

See Tool 1A.10 on primegenesis.com/tools for a discussion of culture across all the steps of onboarding.

Adjust to the Inevitable Surprises

John Wooden, the legendary coach of University of California at Los Angeles (UCLA) basketball, whose teams won an astounding 10 U.S. National Collegiate Athletic Association championships, said: "Things turn out the best for the people who make the best of the ways things turn out." As a leader, it is up to you to make the best of how things turn out. No matter how well you have planned your transition over the first 100 days, no matter how disciplined you are in your follow-up, some things will be different than you expected. Often, your ability to keep moving forward while reacting to the unexpected or the unplanned will be the determining factor in whether your transition is a deemed a success or failure.

One of the main advantages to starting early and deploying the building blocks of tactical capacity quickly is that you and your team will be ready that much sooner to adjust to changing circumstances and surprises. Remember, the ability to respond flexibly and fluidly is a hallmark of a team with tactical capacity. The preceding annual/quarterly/monthly meeting schedule will enable your team to recognize and react to the changes that might impact your team over time.

Table 10.2
Change Map

Type	Temporary Impact	Enduring Impact
Minor Change	**Downplay:** Control and stay focused on priorities	**Evolve:** Factor into ongoing team evolution
Major change	**Manage:** Deploy incident Management response plan	**Restart:** Requires a fundamental redeployment

Not all surprises are equal. Your first job is to sort them out to guide your own and your team's response. If it is a minor/inconsequential, temporary blip, keep your team focused on its existing priorities. If it is minor, but enduring, factor it into your ongoing people, plans, and practices evolution.

Major surprises are a different game. If they're temporary, you'll want to move into crisis or incident management. If they're irreversible and enduring, you'll need to react and make some fundamental changes to deal with the new reality. When you're evaluating change, use Table 10.2 to help guide you to an appropriate measured response.

Major but Temporary

Major but temporary surprises start out either good or bad. They don't necessarily stay that way. Just as a crisis handled well can turn into a good thing, a major event handled poorly can easily turn into a serious crisis. The difference comes down to how well you prepared in advance, implemented the response, and learned and improved for the next time. We go into more depth on this in Chapter 14.

Major and Enduring

Major changes that are enduring require a fundamental restart. These can be material changes in things such as customer needs; collaborators' direction; competitors' strategies; or the economic, political, or social environment in which you operate. They can be internal changes, such as reorganizations, acquisitions, or spin-offs; getting a new boss; or your boss getting a new boss.

Whatever the change, if it's major and enduring, hit a restart button. Go right back to the beginning, do a full situation analysis, identify the key stakeholders, relook at your message, restart your communication plan, and get your people, plans, and practices realigned around the new purpose. Remember, the fittest adapt best.

Summary and Implications

Your leadership: Assess your own leadership and put in place a plan to make it even better. Get support to implement that plan.

People: Invest in future capability development planning, succession planning, and contingency planning; performance management; and talent reviews annually.

Practices: Milestone Management, Long-Term Planning, and Program Management: Install a cadence to conduct business reviews and longer-term planning processes quarterly and milestone updates monthly. Invest in a program management skill set when the sheer volume of change is stretching the organization beyond its capacity to manage with existing processes.

Culture: Close the gap between today's culture and your target culture by engaging your leadership team and deploying tools that will reinforce and accelerate the change program.

Surprises: Adjust to the inevitable surprises based on the degree and length of their impact.

Finis origine pendet (the end depends on the beginning)—so says the first-century Latin poet Marcus Manilius. In a transition into a new leadership role or team merger, if you do not get the beginning right, the end will be ugly.

Conversely, if you follow this book's framework and take advantage of its advice and tools, you will lead your team to the right place, in the right way, at the right times. If you do this, you will develop trust, loyalty, and commitment—and your team will follow.

By using the proven onboarding methodologies presented in this book to enhance and synchronize your people, plans, and practices, you will build the tactical capacity to inspire and enable others to do their absolute best together, to realize a meaningful and rewarding shared purpose that delivers better results faster than anyone thought possible.

Note the most up-to-date, full, editable versions of all tools are downloadable at primegenesis.com/tools.

Quarterly Reviews

Use this tool and its prototypical agenda to plan out your quarterly meeting cadence.

Topics: Financial results versus plan, prior year, and forecast. Progress against key initiatives

Every quarter:

Prior Quarter Review: Results versus expectations and applicable learning

Current Quarter Update: Track progress and make tactical adjustments

Next Quarter: Confirm implementation details

Two Quarters out: Finalize plans

Three Quarters out: Agree on preliminary plans

Four Quarters out: Agree on priorities

Annual tasks to be covered during the quarterly review process:

Q1: Talent review

Q2: Strategic planning (three-year financial targets)

Q3: Future capability development, succession, and contingency planning

Q4: Next year's operating plans and budgets

Internal Communications

Use this tool to plan your internal communications.

Drive compliance with indirect communication to make people aware.

Encourage contribution with direct communication to help people understand.

Support commitment with emotional communication to fuel belief.

Indirect Communication (through relatively mass media and large-group meetings)

- Daily blog posts
- Weekly updates
- Monthly recaps
- Quarterly and annual reviews
- Special announcements as warranted

Direct Communication (small-group meetings to allow for questions and answers and discussion)

- Daily/Weekly/Monthly staff meetings
- Quarterly reviews
- Special meetings

Emotional Communication (one-on-one to get at emotions)

- Antecedents to prompt important behaviors
- Behaviors
- Consequences of behaviors (positive and negative)

Leverage the ABCDE model to optimize communication effectiveness:

A- Audience: Determine which audience(s) you intend to reach.

B- Behavior: Define the desired behavior from your audience (belief, understanding, commitment).

C- Content: Craft the messages and specific content.

D- Design: Determine manner, mode, and environment for the communication.

E- Evaluation: Measure the effectiveness of the communication in driving the desired behavior(s).

TOOL 10.3

Program Management

Use this tool to help with your program management.

Objectives/Goals: Specific, measurable results (SMART)

Context

- Information that led to the objectives:
- Intent behind the objectives:
- What's going to happen after the objective is achieved:

Resources: Human, financial, and operational resources available to the team. Other teams, groups, and units working in parallel, supporting, or interdependent areas.

Guidelines: What the team can and cannot do with regard to roles and decisions. Interdependencies between the team being chartered and the other teams involved.

Accountability: Structure, update timing, and completion timing.

Roles and Responsibilities: (Responsible, Accountable, Consulted, Informed)

TOOL 10.4

Coaching and Support

Use this framework to evolve your leadership and potentially enter into a coaching/support relationship.

1. Begin with the end in mind: objectives, goals, end state
2. Understand current reality: the current state
3. Agree on strengths and barriers: what's working/causing the gap
4. Plan to bridge gaps: Attitude? Relationships? Behaviors?
5. Implement, monitor, adjust: changes and impact

Tactically:

Retrospective coaching: Situation? Action? Result? What worked well? What worked less well? Implications?

Prospective coaching: End in mind? Situation? Barrier/problem to solve? How to close gap/solve problem?

Tool:

Utilize 360-degree feedback or a more detailed diagnostic tool to determine areas for improvement

- Leverage trusted third party (HR, coach, consultant, mentor no longer in the same organization)
- Trusted third party engages and gains feedback from direct reports, peers, and boss(es)
- Seek feedback on areas to *keep*, *stop*, and *start* doing to increase effectiveness
- Debrief with third party and boss to determine areas of focus, actions, and coaching routine

Special Circumstances

CHAPTER 11

Manage Your New Board

At their core, boards of directors provide oversight, approve the most material decisions, and advise, whereas management has accountability for strategy, operations, and the organization. The best do these together, complementing and supporting the other's roles and strengths. So easy to say. So hard to get right across different types of boards and organizations.[1]

Board Accountabilities and Responsibilities

As a general principle, a board of directors of a for-profit company in the United States is charged with "maximizing the value of the corporation for the benefit of its shareholders."[2] Boards do this by making decisions and providing oversight in compliance with the directors' duties of care and loyalty. Essentially, this means board members must

---

[1] George Bradt, 2015, "How Boards and Management Best Create Value Together," *Forbes*, April 29.
[2] Corporate Director's Guidebook – American Bar Association. Note some U.S. state statutes allow the board to consider the impact of decisions on the community, employees, and so forth and that there are statutes that, so long as shareholders are told up front, allow trade-off of profit for social good. Similarly, European boards serve "stakeholders" versus "shareholders."

exercise good business judgment in the best interests of the organization across governance, strategic, organizational, and operational processes without regard to personal gain as they:

- (*Governance*) Set broad policies and objectives and oversee rigorous processes taking into consideration compliance, finance, management, legal, and risk issues.

- (*Strategic*) Approve strategic plans, major expenditures and transactions, and the acquisition or disposal of material assets or the entity itself.

- (*Organizational*) Hire and fire the CEO. Approve top management appointments and succession, and compensation plans for the CEO and top management. Evolve and strengthen the board itself.

- (*Operational*) Approve plans to obtain required financial resources, annual plans, and budgets and oversee efforts to sustain and enhance the organization's public image.

Applicability Across Different Types of Boards

Public boards represent the shareholders of public companies. They are subjected to the strictest regulations and scrutiny and spend most of their time as boards involved in oversight and decision-making. Management needs to give members of these boards what they require for oversight and decision-making and then to implement.

Private fiduciary boards represent the owners of non-public companies. While they are not subject to all the public regulations and scrutiny, they are subject to many of them and must provide oversight and decision-making in the interests of all the owners.

Private nonfiduciary boards primarily have advisory and oversight roles as the controlling owners maintain the fiduciary responsibility. Those owners may be private equity firms, families, or individuals and their organizations may be operating with different levels of maturity and different issues and opportunities. Care should be taken lest the "directors" take on fiduciary duties. Management needs to pay attention to the shadow boards behind the official boards to make sure they are implementing the right decisions.

Nonprofit boards serve different roles in addition to their fiduciary duties potentially including fundraising, contributing personal time, making connections for the organization with strategic partners, and acting as advisors or representatives of critical stakeholders.

Creating Value Together

As PrimeGenesis partner Rob Gregory says, "If management and the board are on the same page with a shared vision as the underlying foundation for understanding respective roles and responsibilities, most relationship issues can be managed." That shared vision of what will happen and when helps clarify when board members are making decisions versus overseeing and supporting. Along the way, management needs to know when, why, and how to provide board members with the tools and support they need to do their jobs.

In the best value-creating partnerships, management appreciates its board members' oversight, approval, and advisory roles and provides those board members with the information they need to do those well. For their part, board members are careful not to confuse oversight, approval, or advice with delegated accountability and responsibility and let management manage.

With that in mind, an ideal board's composition complements management's strengths in leadership and industry as well as functional expertise (technology, intellectual property, finance, audit, risk management, marketing, government relations, and human resources, particularly compensation) and geographic/global perspective. Arguably some of the most important assets boards can acquire, develop, and dispose of are the board members themselves.

The key to creating value together is a close partnership between the board and management. To achieve that:

1. Ensure everyone shares the same vision of success, major milestones, and end-game timing.

2. Clarify roles, responsibilities, interdependencies, and how best to operate together.

3. Assemble and nurture complementary strengths on board and management teams.

FIGURE 11.1   Board Roles and Management

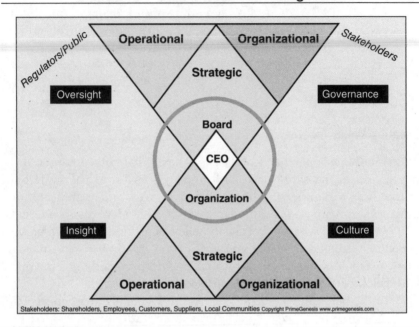

Stakeholders: Shareholders, Employees, Customers, Suppliers, Local Communities Copyright PrimeGenesis www.primegenesis.com

There no single right way to divide responsibilities between owners, chairs, CEOs, COOs, and the rest of the executive team. Authority is delegated. That delegation depends on the business context and confidence the leaders have in one another (Figure 11.1).

Having said that, Rita's Italian Ice and Falconhead Capital—the investment firm that owned a controlling interest of the company—developed an effective working model. Rita's executive board chair Mike Lorelli explains how they broke down the roles:

The executive chair takes the lead on:

- Running the board of directors
- Dealing with external funding (investors and lenders)
- Joint venture pursuits and relations
- Compensation practices
- Management development
- CEO succession
- Strategic plan guidance

The CEO takes the lead on running the company, across its:

- Strategic process
- Operating process
- Organizational process

When it works, it works great. Think about how Bill Gates backed off and gave Steve Ballmer room to run Microsoft and how, in turn, Satya Nadella successfully transitioned into the role in 2014. But when it doesn't work, the pain and suffering are spread across all of those people who are trying to follow their leaders. If leaders can't sort through their own responsibilities, they have no chance of providing clear direction to anyone else.

In summary, here is a rough guide for dividing responsibilities between an executive chair and CEO:

1. Owners delegate authority to boards.

Chairs or lead directors run boards. (This is the only responsibility of a non-executive chair. Executive chairs are employees of the companies by definition and take more active roles in supporting the CEO's leadership of the company.)

2. CEOs run companies.

3. COOs, CFOs, CHROs, and others help CEOs run core operating, strategic, and organizational processes.

4. People lean in or out depending on their confidence in the ability of the people they have chosen to deal with.

Treat this as a general framework. What really matters is role clarity and leadership that inspires, enables, and empowers others.

Deloitte's Chief Executive Program published a paper in 2019 on "Seven steps to a more strategic board."[3] Its insights are well worth reading. They did, however, bury the lead. The seven steps add up to

---

[3] Vincent Firth, Maureen Bujno, Benjamin Finzi, and Kathy Lu, 2019, "Seven Steps to a More Strategic Board," *Deloitte Insights*, July 8.

the importance of CEOs taking a leadership role in managing boards and building relationships rooted in "mutual respect, trust and support." That's the lead.[4]

Deloitte's seven steps:

1. CEOs, it's really up to you. Take an active role in board management.
2. Be fearlessly transparent. Be open and humble.
3. Take advantage of tension. Grow through debate.
4. Facilitate the board experience, not just the board meeting. Build relationships over time.
5. Curate information, and then curate it again. Give enough, but not too much information.
6. To chair or not to chair? Think about it very carefully. Choose your level of influence.
7. Say your piece on board composition. Build the right board over time.

Private equity boards can have a different feel compared to public company boards, for a few reasons.

First, a majority of board seats and votes are held by members of the private equity firms themselves—they have recommended and approved the investment in the company and often have a sizable personal stake in the outcome.

Second, there is a greater-than-average urgency around results delivery, reflecting the intention to monetize the investment via a sale or IPO within a relatively short period of time.

Third, they've performed the detailed due diligence and done the work to develop the investment thesis, giving them an unusually intimate perspective on specific priorities and approaches to create growth and value in the business.

All of this adds up to a greater level of intensity and desire for your private equity board to engage in the strategic, operational, and

---

[4] George Bradt, 2019, "How to Build Mutual Respect, Trust and Support Between CEOs and Boards per Deloitte," *Forbes*, July 9.

organizational processes of the business. Does this mean you yield and abrogate responsibility for these processes? No. Does it mean you need to be prepared for it? By all means, yes.

Relationships

Meanwhile, all the clarity of process and role delineation will go for naught if you don't build strong, trusted relationships with each member of your board.

Relationships rooted in "mutual respect, trust, and support" don't happen by mistake. They are built together, deliberately, and over time.

Start with the Lead Director

The lead director's main role is to help the CEO manage the board; therefore, invest in this relationship as your priority. As you solidify this relationship, the lead director can be a resource to help you nurture the rest.

Respect

Be respectful of board members' context, strengths, and roles. Give them every reason to respect you. Respect their time and help them learn enough to contribute as effectively and efficiently as possible.

Per one director, "Too much information can be just as bad as too little information." You can keep boards in the dark by giving them too little information too infrequently. You can accomplish the same end by drowning them with a board book on an iPad "and secretly hidden are 1,800 pages."

At the same time, beware of complacency. What starts off as an apparently "easy" relationship—where challenges are minimal and approvals are smooth—can devolve if taken for granted. Make strong communication a habit, spend personal time getting to know directors, and dig deep to understand perspectives and motivations.

When onboarding new directors, collaborate with the lead director and your team to develop a plan covering:

- Learning the business: external and internal context, priority issues, upcoming decision points
- Building relationships: exposure to other board members and management team members
- Board processes and roles: clarity on board processes and what's expected in their role

Once board members are in place, often it is helpful to use a what, so what, now what approach. Present an executive summary—details of what, where, when, why, who, and how things are evolving. Lead with the "now what" you're asking the board member to do. Do you want them thinking guidance, advice, and input or thinking governance, compliance, and approval? Be specific on your ask for input or approval.

Then give them your perspective on "so what." These are your conclusions from the information that leads to your request for input or approval.

Finally, organize the backup. "What" data and information are needed by the board members that want to dig deeper into the basis of your assumptions and logic.

Another way to respect board members is not to surprise them. No one likes surprises that make them look stupid, weak, or ill-informed. Build relationships with them. Keep them informed. No excuses.

Finally, do the same future capability planning with your board that you're doing with the rest of the organization. Figure out what capabilities you're going to need in the future and then create and implement a plan to recruit board members with the talents you need. Along the way, help them acquire the knowledge and practice the skills they'll need to optimize their contributions.

Trust

On one level, this is pretty straightforward. Be trustworthy and have a bias to trust them. This is one of the keys to taking advantage of constructive disagreements. As Deloitte put it:

"With a strong partnership between the board and CEO, what at first may feel like difficult conversations can become revelatory dialogues, surfacing ideas and insights that might otherwise stay buried from a desire to smooth tension and maintain civility stay buried from a desire to smooth tension and maintain civility."[5]

Support

One of the authors of the Deloitte paper, Maureen Bujno, says the key to gaining respect, trust, and support lies in CEOs being "fearlessly transparent" and "open to soliciting input."[6] Yet Stanford Business School ex-dean Robert Joss said at a JD Power and Associates conference in 2002, "Only 20% of leaders have the confidence to be open to input."[7] Be part of that 20 percent.

Help board members know when to provide guidance, advice, and input and when to exercise their fiduciary obligations around governance, compliance, and approvals.

Consider Bryan Smith's five levels of persuasion in *The Fifth Discipline Fieldbook:*[8]

1. **Tell:** Not a lot of discussion. I'm in charge. You are directed.

2. **Sell:** I know I'm right and am going to persuade you to buy my idea.

3. **Test:** I've got a trial balloon that I'd like to run by you. I'm interested in what you think. I want to gauge your reaction.

4. **Consult:** I've got an idea that I'd like you to help me improve. I'm open to your input and seek it.

5. **Co-create:** Let's solve this problem together, starting with a blank page as partners.

---

[5] Firth et al., "Seven Steps."

[6] Ibid.

[7] Robert Joss to George Bradt, verbal correspondence, August 15, 2002.

[8] Peter Senge, Art Kleiner, Charlotte Roberts, Richard B. Ross, and Bryan J. Smith, 1994, *The Fifth Discipline Fieldbook: Strategies and Tools for Building a Learning Organization.* Doubleday.

Let's begin by taking two approaches off the table. It's generally not helpful for a CEO to try to *tell* their board what to do. It's also not a good idea to *co-create* with the board. (They want you to lead and come to them with potential solutions and your best current thinking.) So, you are left with *sell, test,* and *consult* as the best ways to persuade your board.

Ken Chenault's Two-Look Approach

Former American Express CEO Ken Chenault liked to give his board of directors two looks at any major idea. This gave them time to reflect on the idea, talk among themselves, and come back to him one-on-one before deciding.

Step 1: Seek their input. Then go away so they talk among themselves or with others or give you an off-the-record perspective.

Step 2: Take into account their input, encourage debate, and seek their approval on your recommended path forward.

The Board Two-Step

By combining Smith's *sell, test,* and *consult* persuasions with Chenault's two-look approach, a very effective way to manage your board emerges (Tool 11.1).

Here are the steps:

Step 1: Consult or Test

If you do your job right here, your board members relax. If they know they don't have to make a decision, they can focus on helping you. Instead of your ideas being a proposal, they represent your current best thinking for others to build on—without having to judge you or your best current thinking.

Go Away

Giving the board time and space to mull things over is important. It allows them to come back to you with their real thinking or lobby each other.

Step 2: Sell

Note this is "sell," not "railroad." You will have gotten input along the way. Share the concerns you've heard so the board can discuss— and then seek their approval to your recommended path forward.

Works with Senior Leadership, Too

Although we developed this approach for boards, it works with all sorts of groups. It is a good way to separate out input from direction. It is almost always a good idea to clarify if you are seeking or providing input (after which the person receiving the input gets to make a decision) or direction (a decision to be implemented by others).

Summary and Implications

Boards of directors provide oversight, approve the most material decisions, and advise, while management has accountability for strategy, operations, and the organization. As CEO, follow Deloitte's seven steps. The Board Two-Step can help a lot here.

Step 1: Seek their input. Then go away so they can talk among themselves or with others or give you an off-the-record perspective.

Step 2: Take into account their input, encourage debate, and seek their approval to your recommended path forward.

Take time to proactively manage your transition into board management. You'll need to plan—and stick to—a schedule that allows for more time to build and maintain these new relationships and collaborate with your lead director on managing the board to support the desired outcomes for the organization.

Focus on relationships, starting with the lead director, who can help you manage the board.

Note the most up-to-date, full, editable versions of all tools are downloadable at primegenesis.com/tools.

TOOL 11.1

The Board Two-Step

Before Step 1, prepare the board by giving them the appropriate amount of information in advance. Think Goldilocks: not too little and not too much.

Step 1: *Consult* or *test* with the board. Be clear you are seeking their input, not decision.

Then go away. Give the board time and space to mull things over and have one-on-one conversations with you.

Step 2: *Sell*. Lead the board through a final conversation and seek their decision.

CHAPTER 12

Lead Through Mergers and Acquisitions

Those leading through a merger, acquisition, or the like do so to accelerate value creation. They look for revenues to double or more on the way to returning many multiples of their initial investments. Maybe you're driving or leading the investment. Maybe you're leading the business itself or playing a supporting role. In any case, you need a leadership playbook for the merger or acquisition.

This chapter describes the 14 steps we've used as investors, leaders, and supporters. Our overarching approach is to work through customers, people, and costs—in that order. First, figure out how you're going to win with customers. Then build the leadership and team required for that. Fund those efforts with your cost-cutting.

This is how we've created value faster against a backdrop of others failing to deliver the desired results 83 percent of the time. In a *Harvard Business Review* article, Kenny Graham noted that "between 70 and 90 percent of acquisitions fail"[1] and a KPMG M&A study found that 17 percent of deals added value while 30 percent produced no discernible difference and 53 percent destroyed value.[2]

---

[1] Graham, Kenny, 2020, "Don't Make This Common M&A Mistake," *Harvard Business Review*, March 16.
[2] KPMG Mergers and Acquisitions: Global Research Report, 1999.

The Steps

1. Start with the **investment case**—the heart of your playbook.

    Be clear on what you want out of an acquisition or merger, how it would fit with what you've already got, and what you're willing to give up to get it. Then broaden your perspective to look at different possibilities before narrowing on the few best candidates and putting together investment cases for them.

    Before you attempt to acquire and integrate another entity, it's best to know your own entity first. When leaders have in-depth knowledge of their own strategic, organizational, and operational processes as well as their culture, they are far better positioned to leverage and blend the combined strengths of their own and other entities.

    Similarly, understand the business context in which you're operating. Your strategy revolves around a set of choices about the markets, segments, and customers you'll serve. Know and understand them better than anyone else.

    And if you can't define the value creation you are seeking, it doesn't exist. Define desired outcomes for your markets, segments, customers, organization, shareholders, and your people—as well as how new value is going to be created through the investment case fundamentals:

    a. Pay fair value for what company is currently worth.

    b. Grow topline (organically and inorganically) with customers through people.

    c. Make operational/operational engineering improvements, cutting costs.

    d. Invest in topline and bottom-line enablers to accelerate progress.

    e. Improve cash flows and pay down debt.

    f. Exit or recapitalize when this round of value creation is done.

2. Do **the deal** in a way that reduces your risk of being part of the 83 percent of mergers and acquisitions that fail to deliver the desired results.

   The first of the many investments you need to get a return on is the purchase price. Since only 17 percent of deals add value and 53 percent destroy it, it is better not to pay enough and lose a deal than to overpay and win one of the 53 percent that destroy value.

   The starting point for your deal should be a fair value for what the company is currently worth based on current cash flows. This would reward the seller for what they've built and keep all future value creation. Of course, in the real world, others may be willing to give the seller a portion of the estimated future value. Couple that with some over-estimation of future value creation and ego and it's easy to see how people bid more than they should to "win" bidding contests.

   Your real investment is different depending upon how you finance the deal. Consider options for funding beyond cash, including equity; seller funding or earnout; debt in the form of loans, bonds, credit lines, bridge financing, mezzanine, or subordinated debt; among others.

3. Do your **due diligence** on the key ingredients for success.

   Due diligence is your chance to check your assumptions. If you put a breakup fee in the deal, you did that to allow you to walk away if appropriate. Historically, 83 percent of the time others should have done that.

   Learn as much as you can about the strategic, organizational, and operational processes and culture of the entity you're acquiring. Don't just take third parties' opinions; be active in learning as much as you can . . . as soon as you can.

   a. Check your assumptions about the synergy value creators that can enhance competitive advantages, increase impact, and enable top-line growth.

   b. Check your assumptions about synergistic cost-reductions that can fuel investment in the value creators.

    c. Check your assumptions about cultural compatibility. Because if you can't make this work, nothing else matters.

    d. Then make a go or no-go decision being clear on the advantage of cutting your losses before they become material.

Consider using the BRAVE tool below to document the results of your "culture due diligence." Define where your organization sits on the spectrum for each element, and then do the same for the target company you are assessing. This exercise will help identify cultural differences that may be cultural divides if not addressed.

4. Start setting up **cultural integration** well before the deal closes to help your new people become valued participants in the new organization.

A merger is not a friendship. It is not dating. It is marriage. So treat it as such. A detailed integration plan that spans across organizational, operational, strategic, and cultural issues is essential. We've all seen organizations acquire other organizations and then run them as wholly owned, separate entities. You can't possibly realize synergies out of separate organizations. Synergies must be created together by teams looking beyond themselves to new problems they can solve for others.

The root cause of many mergers' success or failure is culture. Manage that cultural transformation actively and purposefully. Have a cultural transformation plan in place. (Refer to Chapter 4 for insights on how to evolve culture.) When you merge cultures well, value is created. When you don't, value is destroyed.

Choose the behaviors, relationships, attitudes, values, and environment that will make up your new culture. As you're choosing key leaders and broader team, keep in mind that you are inviting people into the new culture, noting who really accepts your invitation in what they say, do, and are.

5. Choose your **key leaders** before the close or kickoff: Share the vision and get them aligned—including standing up an integration office.

The only thing you can do all by yourself is fail. Successfully chasing synergy requires an interdependent team with its members all paddling in the same direction. This must start before the start.

Table 12.1
Culture Due Diligence

	Acquiror					Target					
	1	2	3	4	5	1	2	3	4	5	
Environment—*Where to play*											
Workplace											
Remote–virtual, open, informal											In-person, closed, formal
Work–life balance											
Health and wellness first											Near-term productivity first
Enablers:											
Human/interpersonal/societal											Technical/mechanical/scientific
Values—What matters and why											
Focus											
Doing good for others/ESG											Doing good for selves/good at
Learning:											
Open/shared/value diversity											Directed/individual/single-minded
Risk appetite:											
Risk more/gain more (confidence)											Protect what is/minimize mistakes
Attitude—*How to win*											
Strategy:											
Premium price/service/innovation											Low cost/low-service/minimum viable

(continued)

(continued)

	Acquiror					Target					
	1	2	3	4	5	1	2	3	4	5	
Environment—*Where to play*											
Focus:											
Divergence from competitors											Convergence on market leader
Posture:											
Proactive/breakthrough innovation											Responsive/reliable steady progress
Relationships—*How connect*											
Power, decision-making:											
Diffused/debated											Controlled/monarchical
Diversity, equity, and inclusion:											
All welcome, valued, respected											Bias to work with people just like us
Communication, controls											
Informal/verbal/face to face											Formal/directed/written
Behaviors—*What Impact*											
Working units:											
One org. Interdependent teams											Independent individuals, units, groups
Discipline:											
Fluid/flexible (guidelines)											Structured/disciplined (policies)
Delegation											
Inspire, enable, empower											Narrow task-focused direction

FIGURE 12.1   Core Focus

Flexibility

	DESIGN	SERVICE
Core	**DESIGN**	**SERVICE**
Culture	Learning & Enjoyment	Purpose & Caring
Organization	**SPECIALIZED**	**DECENTRALIZED**
Leader	Enable - Principles	Experience - Guidelines
Operations	**FREEING SUPPORT**	**GUIDED ACCOUNTABILITY**

Independence ◄———— Purpose ————► Interdependence

	PRODUCE	DELIVER
Core	**PRODUCE**	**DELIVER**
Culture	Results & Authority	Order & Safety
Organization	**HIERARCHY**	**MATRIX**
Leader	Enforce - Policies	Enroll - Team Charters
Operations	**COMMAND & CONTROL**	**SHARED RESPONSIBILITY**

Stability

Select "new" management team members and then pull them together to align on the core focus of the new organization: design, production, delivery, or service (Figure 12.1). That choice dictates the nature of your culture, organization, and ways of working.

6. **Plan** for success with your leaders, focusing on customers, people, and costs—in that order.

Preparation breeds confidence. Creating your 100-day and 365-day plans in advance allows you to be ahead of the curve and to adjust to the inevitable surprises that come your way. Think burning imperative. This is where you'll want the combined entity's new leaders to co-create a plan to compete and win in the market, in the segments, and with customers you choose to serve and how to enroll the rest of the organization.

Move through a situation assessment including a synergy evaluation to thinking through the value proposition, and then integrated project planning steps to accelerate your strategic, organizational, and operating processes.

Then map your new stakeholders including the broader team. Clarify your going-in hypothetical message. Map out the announcement, preclose/prestart meetings, Day One, and early days.

7. Manage the **politics**: What current and new leaders need to know organizationally and personally.

Inevitably, some will choose to disengage from the new venture. Some will watch and comply—for a while. Some will contribute. Some will commit and champion the cause. You're never going to get the disengaged to commit. Instead, try to move everyone one step. Enroll the champions to help pull up the contributors, and the contributors to help pull up the watchers. Help those disengaged find other causes to which they can commit.

Chances are, you missed something (or a lot of somethings) during due diligence. Soon after the close, invest in a series of two-way learning sessions across the new organization. This will accelerate team-building, highlight unforeseen challenges in integration, and at the same time excite the combined team about the possibilities and payoffs of combining efforts.

8. Avoid early land mines with a well-crafted **announcement cascade**.

Everything communicates. Everything you say and do and don't say and don't do. This is especially true on the Day One when a merger closes or teams are combined. Everyone will have the same question, and only one question. Whatever they say, all they want to know is "What does this mean for me?" You and your leadership team must be prepared to answer this question and address specific questions around reporting lines ("do I have a different boss?"), responsibilities ("are my priorities changing?"), and compensation ("help me understand any changes in salary, bonus structure, and benefits").

Do you see what's happening here? We're eight steps into this and just getting to Day One. This is the M&A equivalent of the carpenter's "measure twice and cut once." Preparation is key.

9. Get the right **people** in the right roles much faster than you think you should.

Strengthen the organization: acquiring, developing, encouraging, planning, and transitioning talent:

- Acquire: Recruit, attract, and onboard the right people with the right talent.

- Develop: Assess and build skills, knowledge, experience, and craft.

- Encourage: Direct, support, recognize, and reward.
- Plan: Monitor, assess, and plan career moves over time.
- Transition: Migrate to different roles as appropriate.

Take a hard look at the combined organization's skills and capabilities through the lens of the new core focus and strategy to determine if any critical capability sets are missing or misaligned. Look not only at the people, plans, and practices, but pay particular attention to how well you are performing in the markets, segments, and customers you've decided to pursue. Quickly move to bridge any gaps that exist.

Start by defining the right structure and roles to execute on your mission. Be specific about talent, knowledge, skill, experience, and craft requirements for success in each key role, and then match them with the right people.

- *Innate talent*—either born with or not
- *Learned knowledge*—from books, classes, or training
- *Practiced skills*—from deliberate repetition
- *Hard-won experience*—digested from real-world mistakes
- *Apprenticed craft*—absorbed from masters with artistic care and sensibilities

10. Deploy the fundamentals of **change management** to inspire, enable, and empower others.

    Now that they have had their "What about me?" question answered, pivot to inspiring, enabling, and empowering them to work effectively together and deliver on the promises of the combination.

    All lasting change is cultural change in attitudes, relationships, and behaviors following a point of inflection change in environment/situation or ambition/objectives.

    To support growth, invest in the team's tactical capacity—the ability to translate strategies into tactical actions decisively, rapidly, and effectively, with high-quality responsiveness under difficult, changing conditions.

11. Leverage **cost-cutting** as an enabler while jump-starting your operational, executional, and financial processes.

    The operational processes that could deliver results before your merger or acquisition are not going to be adequate to deliver the post point of inflection results. If they were, you wouldn't need to go through the point of inflection. Work through how to maintain and evolve the best of the current processes while layering the new required processes on top to deliver the needed cost reductions and fuel revenue growth.

    Essentially, you're going to need to craft, implement, and manage four plans concurrently:

    - Resource allocation and plan (requirements, sources, application): Human, financial, technical, operational

    - Rules of engagement across critical business drivers

    - Action plan (near-term and long-term): Actions, measures, milestones/timing, accountabilities, linkages

    - Performance management plan: Operating/financial performance standards and measures

12. Keep going with ongoing **communication**—both ways—because your communication campaign never ends, you can never overcommunicate.

    It's all about treating people with respect. On any communication, make sure those emotionally impacted hear one-on-one to respect their emotions; and make sure those directly impacted hear in a small-enough group to be able to ask questions.

    You'll want to communicate clearly, often, individually, emotionally, rationally, inspirationally, and globally using multiple methods. Focus on building relationships with the new team members early. Enhance relationships within the existing team. Never stop listening. Always keep the team engaged and communicate:

    - Long-term issues and opportunities should come from senior leadership at least quarterly about organization-wide priorities and results.

- Mid-term issues and opportunities should come from middle management on monthly progress on major programs.

- Short-term issues and opportunities should come from direct supervisors with weekly progress on projects and daily progress on tasks.

13. **Adjust** along the way: How to recognize, prioritize, and make the right moves to realize the investment case.

    Implement systems to track, assess, adjust, daily/weekly/monthly/quarterly/annually: Don't confuse communicating with operating cadences. Avoid the public company sprint to do things just ahead of quarterly earnings calls, instead, staying ahead of the curve at all times.

    - Balanced scorecard: destination, objectives, strategic links, initiatives, measures by

    - Financial (e.g., revenue, cash flow, EBITDA, ROI)

    - Customer (e.g., sales from new products, on-time delivery, share, customer concentration)

    - Internal business processes (e.g., cycle time, unit cost, yield, NPD)

    - Learning and growth (e.g., time to market, product life cycle)

14. Prepare for the **next chapter,** successfully acquiring others—or a sale or liquidity event.

    This is about preparing for further growth/transformation, the next exit, or other "event" as a platform company or bait for strategic buyer. When preparing for an exit, get the story right:

    - Strategically: Organic revenue growth | Other M&A

    - Organizationally: Buyable management team | Capabilities valuable to others

    - Operationally: Buyable infrastructure (Assets, data, IT systems, financial reporting) | Processes | New product development capabilities

    - Personally: Making yourself invaluable to the next owners

Yes. You matter. What really matters is how you influence others and the impact you all make together. Do start with the context and industry landscape. Do align people, plans, and practices around a shared purpose to create commercial and other value. If you've read this far, you know we believe you should do the required cost-cutting. Do it to free up the resources you need to strengthen the combined entity's culture and strategic, organizational, and operational processes. Do that, and your chase for synergy will go well.

CHAPTER 13

Lead a Turnaround

Y ou've been asked to lead a turnaround. First, take a deep breath and understand what you are up against. Your leadership skills are about to be tested. You should be excited about the possibilities and concerned about the risks as 70 percent of transformations fail to deliver desired results.[1]

Before we jump in too deep, note that we've chosen to use the term *turnaround* to refer to a range of critical transitions where rapid change is called for, whether a *transformation* ("thorough, dramatic, lasting change in form"), an *acceleration* (need to get "un-stuck" and go faster in the same direction), or an actual *turnaround* ("an abrupt or unexpected change, especially one that results in a more favorable situation").

Turnarounds are more prevalent than you might think, driven by external and internal factors. External forces include rapidly emerging new technologies, geopolitical instabilities, global health crises, regulatory changes, rapidly shifting consumer demand, changing economies, and swift emergence of well-funded new competitors. Internally, increased presence of activist shareholders and accelerating growth in private equity transactions have led to dramatically raised ownership ambitions and expectations for business performance.

---

[1] Rajiv Chandran et al., 2015, "Ascending to the C-Suite," McKinsey Insights, April.

These critical transitions are particularly risky and challenging when a leader enters a new role and the organization has yet to realize the nature of the situation. Turnarounds exacerbate all of the issues we've discussed thus far. More will be required of you. As you step into the leadership role, be aware of these six critical success factors:

1. **Call it and communicate it.** There is a lingering impression that organizations or teams slowly evolve into turnaround situations over time. That may have been true at one time, but the stark reality of today's global economy is that yesterday's star division quickly can become today's turnaround situation. If you have identified a turnaround situation (don't always be sure that the company will do it for you), then you must declare it as such and make sure every one of your key shareholders understands.

   You may need to declare the turnaround before it's obvious from published data on results. Turn up the heat by highlighting the private, internal stories of failure the team relates to emotionally (loss of a major customer, departure of top talent) that indicate decline. Provide sufficient time for team members to absorb the information and accept the implications. But do it fast. You must lead differently in a turnaround situation. By calling it and communicating it you are signaling to your team and the organization that change is coming and fast!

2. **Understand and align expectations.** It's important to get clear on the turnaround expectations up front. And everyone up, down, and across (internally and externally) must be aligned with those expectations. Often, a turnaround situation is surrounded by panic and emotions.

   Often the expectation from leaders is to "get that division back on track." That is not an expectation, it's an unclear wish. You must seek and, in fact, often be the one that defines clarity on the precise expectations for the turnaround and subsequent recovery. How is recovery defined? Is it more revenue growth, higher market share, cost reduction? Or a series of items that mean you need to dig deeper and rethink your core beliefs and transform your operations and organization? You must know the answer and make sure everyone is aligned.

3. **Move quickly and decisively.** You will want to follow the same onboarding steps that we've laid in previous chapters; but you'll want to move quicker wherever you can.

Remember our ACES analysis in Chapter 2 that guides you on how to engage with your new organization? In a turnaround scenario your choices are limited to two. You'll either converge and evolve (very quickly) or shock.

Your burning imperative is even more essential. It must be decisive, clearly articulated, precisely aligned with expectations, and clearly understood by all.

Do your role match as quickly as the situation allows (realizing you may need new roles and new players in those roles). And give even greater emphasis to your milestone management process and the frequency of checkpoints early on.

4. **Overcommunicate.** It is essential to communicate early and often with your stakeholders and especially your team. The nature of the turnaround is to generate surprises. You'll be evaluating and possibly pivoting more than usual, and you'll have to double your efforts to communicate early and often across your key stakeholder list. If things are worse than expected, let everyone know early. Bad news doesn't get better with age.

On the contrary, don't let the fast pace of the turnaround environment bury the good things that are happening. Look for ways to celebrate victories and desired behaviors. Weekly town halls with your team in the early months is often a smart thing to do.

Finally, listen like you've never listened before. Your team is in the trenches, and they will be able to share game-changing insights and information that can speed the turnaround. Frequently ask and listen. Then do it again.

5. **Overinvest for innovation.** Do not skimp on resources. You'll have to invest to change the underperforming nature of the business. Those investments might be new people, technology, equipment. But whatever they are, don't hamper the turnaround by being slow to make essential investments.

On the other hand, you may also have to make tough decisions that will incur significant expenses, such as closing plants, relocating offices, letting people go, or other restructuring costs. Make those choices as quickly as possible.

Pay particular attention to investing sufficient resources on innovation. Innovation in all forms (product, channel, supply chain, people) is the soul of a successful turnaround, giving you the chance to deliver results that will last. Innovation will help you do things better, quicker, and cheaper or even completely change the playing field in your favor. Make sure you're investing for innovation.

6. **Enter humble. Leave confident.** Turnaround situations are fraught with emotion. Nobody likes to fail. Nobody likes to make public mistakes. If you've been asked to lead a turnaround, everyone will know the reason for the leadership change. Enter the situation humbly and respectfully and don't let the need for speed cause you to gloss over the embedded emotions, heartfelt disappointments, or lingering embarrassments that may exist within your team.

Do not cast aspersions on the previous team or highlight their failures as it will only undermine your leadership, rub salt in fresh wounds, and generate ill will, none of which are beneficial to you or the team. Instead, enter humbly with compassion. Quickly share the picture of success, ensure every member of the team feels part of the turnaround and knows what is in it for them. If you do that and follow the steps laid out in this chapter, you will quickly build trust and confidence from the team and operating momentum in the business.

With all that in mind, you can accelerate through a turnaround situation by deploying five building blocks (Figure 13.1).

1. **Define catalysts.** Assess the changes in the situation. *What* has not and what has changed and why? What is the catalyst driving the need for change? *So what* are the implications of that? *Now what* must you do?

    a. Understand catalysts for change (internally, such as changes in ambition, or chinks in the armor on culture and talent man-

FIGURE 13.1   Building Blocks

Assess & Plan	Strategy	Organization	Operations
Change catalysts:	Overarching strategy	Future capability plan	Leadership approach
Situation/ambitions	Strategic priorities	Immediate role sort	Management cadence
Best current thinking	Cultural changes	Leadership mindset	Incentives
	Ongoing purpose-driven **learning & communication**		

agement, and/or externally in customer dynamics, competition, supply chain, or conditional changes, such as regulatory?) Be sure understanding and buy-in are broad-based.

b. Build on best current thinking on required changes to mission, vision, goals, objectives, strategy, culture, organization, and operations. Understand what's already "set," and what needs to be developed.

c. Create a blueprint for ensuring *strategic alignment* of the organization to navigate at this point of inflection.

d. Establish a *transformation office*—hopefully led by someone other than the top leader. This investment will bring focus and rigor to the effort, helping to avoid the tendency to drift back into managing the day-to-day.

Key elements of that function are milestone management (to keep the team accountable, aligned, and delivering) and internal communication (to create a coherent, rigorously managed messaging platform). This kind of structure allows the leader to lead the entire business ("transformation" and otherwise).

For this role, tend toward an individual with deep experience, broad perspective, and interpersonal credibility. You can determine if the role is full-time/stand-alone or built into the priorities of one of your senior leaders. If you choose the latter, be sure to backfill their day-to-day responsibilities so they can spend the majority of their time on the turnaround.

2. **Reset strategy for winning.** Agree on the core focus, or core differentiator of the enterprise, a new overarching strategy, goals, objectives, strategic priorities, enablers, capabilities, and culture. These must be closely linked to your mission and vision, which should also be reviewed for relevance in light of the changes.

a. **Imperative.** Build consensus around context, the core focus of the enterprise, overarching strategy, goals, objectives, strategic priorities, strategic enablers and capabilities, and culture. It's about alignment, focus, expectations, and deliverables and ensuring leadership commitment and capacity to manage.

For the culture shift:

i. Lay out the aspirational attributes.

ii. Determine what to **keep doing/dial up** re: How we lead? How we get work done? How we interact? How we communicate (two-way)?

iii. Determine what to **stop doing** (see previous).

iv. Determine what to **start or change** (see previous).

The capacity to lead is a nontrivial issue for leaders that need to lead a turnaround and continue to run their functions to deliver short-term results. This comes from a combination of will to lead, skill to lead, and time management, and generally requires tighter prioritization, project management support, allocating certain operational responsibilities across the "next level down," and refining functional operating cadences. Ideally, leaders will have confidence that the transformation leadership can be embraced "as part of" their roles—with this extra support.

b. **Transformative communications strategy:** Develop a multi-channel program to communicate change to the organization and enlist deep organizational engagement over an 18-month timeline. Migrate teams along the compliant—contributing—committed spectrum. This is the second part of the pivot, where you will transfer ownership of the transformation to the rest of the organization.

You'll need to provide:

i. Clarity/buy-in/chance to contribute

ii. Discipline on internal communication, connecting the dots across transformation initiatives as well as other key items in the business, balancing the desire to inform without overwhelming the team

iii. An experienced, well-connected, trusted midlevel manager to lead the effort

iv. Ways to reinforce positive behaviors and small (early) wins—getting the organization to believe requires lots of small positive momentum builders that are visible to as many people as possible

   c. **Leadership guidelines:** Along the way:

      i. Create a new model for your leadership team. Create expectations and systems that ensure adequate time is spent on turnaround initiatives. Unify the team with shared understanding, goals, and incentives. Define and reinforce desired behaviors of teamwork, collaboration, and accountability. This group must be in lockstep in order to succeed through the transition.

      ii. Be deliberate. Everything you do and don't do communicates.

     iii. Use your leadership message to frame discussions, announcements, reports, and learnings.

     iv. Invite two-way communication. Be a truly great listener.

      v. "Be–do–say" the core VALUES. Embed in every communication.

     vi. Set a steady communication cadence (what, when, and how).

    vii. Use questions to initiate communication cascade—"Who else needs to know?"

   viii. More communication is always better. Learn to enjoy being the "chief communication officer."

     ix. Be systematic about following up on anything learned in two-way communications.

3. **Reorganize for success.** Create a new organizational structure and future capability plan in line with your new strategy. Do an immediate role sort. Accelerate individual transitions as appropriate. Deploy appropriate frameworks to help guide everyone's thinking.

    Jump-shift the organization to the right specialized, hierarchy, matrix, or decentralized structure and organizational process, scaling up ability to acquire, develop, encourage, plan, and transition people, including (see Chapter 9):

   a. Future capability planning looking at structure and individuals. Often, in turnarounds and similar critical transitions, new roles are called for, in line with market direction or the need to build a new internal capability. Examples are chief customer experience officer, chief innovation officer, chief data officer, chief brand officer, or even chief transformation officer. Consider, and do what's right for your situation.

 b. Succession planning.

 c. Contingency planning.

 d. Immediate role sort. Dramatic business change often calls for new and different ways of thinking. Be vigilant about bringing diverse perspectives into the team, whether through internal promotions, new hires, or temporary expert roles.

 e. Accelerate individual transitions as appropriate.

4. **Intensify operating cadence.** Implement a new approach, flow, and management cadence to track and manage your priorities annually, programs monthly, and projects weekly as appropriate. Ensure your incentives reward desired actions and call out and rectify undesired actions (see Chapters 7–9):

 a. Identify your leadership approach: enabling, enforcing, enrolling, or experience based on the core focus of the business and couple it with the appropriate operational approach (freeing support, command and control, shared responsibility, or guided accountability).

 b. Corresponding management cadence, *milestone* management, and *early win* implementation across quarterly priorities, monthly programs, and weekly projects.

  This is where things start to happen. You can piggyback on the existing milestone management process if it's working or put in place a new one if needed. Identify a process manager/transformation office to manage the process. Provide clarity around:

- **Direction:** objectives, desired results, intent

- **Resources:** human, financial, technical, and operational

- **Bounded authority** to make tactical decisions within strategic guidelines and, yes, boundaries

- **Accountability** and consequences: standards of performance, time expectations, positive and negative consequences of success and failure

The *milestones* must include current projects as well as transformation priorities as there's one leadership team and one business.

Early wins can be found in projects that are given extra resources to deliver them faster. This way, they are not new or special work, just things delivered "early" to give the team confidence in themselves.

Do a step-down process with the few most important initiatives to ensure full team charter, team kick-off, early project milestone management.

To start, track program progress monthly, project progress weekly, task progress daily.

5. **Embed learning and communication.** Deploy a purpose-driven learning and communication effort in line with your new operating flow and management cadence. This is an ongoing effort, not a one-off event.

Accelerating through a strategic turnaround requires step-changes in strategy, organization, and operations, carefully synced together. Those are necessary, but not sufficient unless you also reinvent yourself as a more sophisticated leader as described by John Hillen and Mark Nevins in *What Happens Now?*[2] Hillen and Nevins argue that doing more of the same thing requires increased capacity or complexity while doing different things requires new capabilities or sophistication. If you're growing steadily, you can probably get away with evolving your mechanics, structure, processes, and systems with your technical and functional knowledge. But leading through a turnaround requires new mindsets, capabilities, and behaviors leveraging political, personal, strategic, and interpersonal strengths.

Hillen and Nevins suggest failing leaders add more complexity while more successful leaders add sophistication. One aspect of that sophistication involves applying different mindsets at different times. Different situations require a leader who is chief enabler, enforcer, enroller, or the champion of customer experience.

---

[2] John Hillen, and Mark Nevins, 2018, *What Happens Now?: Reinvent Yourself as a Leader Before Your Business Outruns You*. SelectBooks

Putting this all together leads you back to the core alignment matrices we presented in Chapter 6. Make those choices deliberately and proceed appropriately.

What Does This Mean for Me?

At every stage of a turnaround, every person in your organization and ecosystem will have one question that must be answered before they can pay attention to anything else: "What does this mean for me?" As a leader you must be ready to answer that question early and often. Because that question is a constant, it should drive elements of your communication plan to make sure you are addressing it. Your answer to that question should be found in your burning imperative, mission, vision, values, role match analysis, and the incentives in place to reinforce the desired behaviors. But the answer to that question for each person is intensely personal.

The nature of the turnaround requires you to push your team. It will be fast-paced, dynamic, full of constant adjustments, setbacks, and victories. Along the way, your most important role, once the direction has been set, is to be there and offer support for your team. They are going to need it. If you follow the steps outlined in this chapter and stay aware of and responsive to your team's needs, the chance of you leading a successful turnaround will be greatly enhanced.

Summary and Implications

As you step into the leadership role of a turnaround, be aware of these six critical success factors:

1. Call it and communicate it.
2. Understand and align expectations.
3. Move quickly and decisively.
4. Overcommunicate.
5. Overinvest for innovation.
6. Enter humble. Leave confident.

Then follow these five steps:

1. **Define catalysts.** Assess the changes in the situation and be clear about the catalysts for change.

2. **Reset strategy for winning.** Agree on the core focus of the enterprise, its mission, vision, goals, objectives, a new overarching strategy, strategic priorities, enablers, capabilities, and culture. Understand and plan for the degree of change the new strategy represents.

3. **Reorganize for success.** Create a new organizational structure and future capability plan in line with your new strategy. New roles (permanent and temporary) are likely needed to jump-start and sustain the effort.

4. **Intensify operating cadence.** Implement a new approach, flow, and management cadence to track and manage your priorities annually, programs monthly, and projects weekly as appropriate.

5. **Embed learning and communication.** Deploy a purpose-driven learning and communication effort in line with your new operating flow and management cadence to lead change over an 18-month timeline.

CHAPTER 14

Lead Through a Crisis

A 100-Hour Action Plan.

*T*he *New Leader's 100-Day Action Plan* is a sequential methodology for leaders and their teams to get done in 100 days what normally takes 6–12 months. In a crisis or disaster, this time frame is woefully inadequate as teams need a way to get done in 100 hours what normally takes weeks or months. This requires an iterative instead of sequential approach. That disciplined iteration is detailed below.

Leadership is about inspiring, enabling, and empowering others. Enhance that with the idea from the British philosopher Carveth Read that "it is better to be vaguely right than precisely wrong."[1] Then add Darwin's point that "it is not the strongest of the species that survives, nor the most intelligent, but the one most responsive to change."[2] Add them all up and you get leading through a crisis being about inspiring, enabling, and empowering others to get things vaguely right quickly, and then adapt along the way—with clarity around direction, leadership, and roles.[3]

---

[1] Carveth Read, 1989, "Logic: Deductive and Inductive," Grant Richards, London, June.
[2] Attributed to Charles Darwin.
[3] George Bradt, 2019, "Learnings from Boeing's 737 Max, Coca-Cola, and Procter & Gamble on Crisis Management," *Forbes*, March 21.

This plays out in three steps of a disciplined iteration that should be aligned with the overall purpose:

1. **Prepare in advance.** The better you have anticipated possible scenarios, the more prepared you are and the more confidence you will have when crises strike.

2. **React to events.** The reason you prepared is so that you all can react quickly and flexibly to the situation you face. Don't overthink this. Do what you prepared to do.

3. **Bridge the gaps.** In a crisis, there is inevitably a gap between the desired and current state. Rectify that by bridging those gaps in the:

   - Situation—implement a response to the current crisis
   - Response—improve capabilities to respond to future crises
   - Prevention—reduce the risk of future crises happening

Along the way, keep the ultimate purpose in mind. It needs to inform and frame everything you do over the short-, mid-, and long-term as you lead through a crisis instead of merely out of a crisis. Crises change your organization. Be sure the choices you make during crises change you in ways that move you toward your purpose and aspirational culture and not away from your core vision and values.

Let's delve deeper into each of these key steps (laid out in Tool 14.1).

Prepare in Advance

Preparing in advance is about building general capabilities and capacity—not specific situational knowledge. For the most part, there is a finite set of the most likely and most devastating types of crises and disasters that are worth preparing for. Think them through. Run the drills. Capture the general lessons so people can apply them flexibly to the specific situations they encounter.[4] Have resources ready to be deployed when those disasters strike.

- Establish crisis management protocols, explicitly including early communication protocols
- Identify and train crisis management teams (with clear leadership and roles)
- Pre-position human, financial, and operational resources

Threats may be one or more of the following, often in combination:
- Physical (Top priority. Deal with these first.)
- Reputational (Second priority. Deal with these after physical but before financial threats.)
- Financial (Third priority.)

Physical threats and crises may be:
- Natural: earthquakes, landslides, volcanic eruptions, floods, cyclones, epidemics, and so forth
- Man-made: stampedes, fires, transport accidents, industrial accidents, oil spills, nuclear explosions/radiation, war, deliberate attacks, and so forth

Reputational threats and crises may result from how physical threats and crises are handled. Or they may come from choices made by you or others in your organization, outside interventions, or sudden awareness of things already there that previously went unnoticed.

Financial threats and crises come from disruptions in your value chain. They can be supply or product or resources (including cash), manufacturing, issues, selling or demand disruptions, and service breaks.

Now, back to three things you should do to prepare.

---

[4] John Harrald argues the need for both discipline (structure, doctrine, process) and agility (creativity, improvisation, adaptability). John Harrald, 2006, "Agility and Discipline: Critical Success Factors for Disaster Response," *The ANNALS of the American Academy of Political and Social Science*, 604, 256.

Establish crisis management protocols. Plan who's going to do what when in a crisis. In general, you'll want first responders to deal with immediate physical threats to people and property. They should:

1. Secure the scene to eliminate further threats to others and themselves

2. Provide immediate assistance to those hurt or injured or set up a triage system to focus on those that can most benefit from help

3. Trigger your communication protocols

There are two parts to your communication protocols. Part I protocols deal with physical issues. Part II deals with reputational issues. Part I protocols spell out who gets informed when (with lots of redundant backups built in). These should have a bias to inform more people faster.

Part II protocols are about formal, external communication. At a minimum, the one, single, primary spokesperson (and backup) message and communication points should be crystal clear. It's a good guideline to follow three overarching ideas from the Forbes Agency Council's 13 Golden Rules of PR Crisis Management.

- Develop strong organizational brand culture to ward off self-inflicted crises and be better ready to deal with others.

- Monitor, plan, and communicate, and be ever on the lookout for potential crises. When they hit, be proactive and transparent, get ahead of the story, and be ready for the social media backlash.

- Take responsibility. Own your own crisis in a human way. Seek first to understand, avoiding knee-jerk reactions, apologize, then take action that helps, not fuels the fire.

Identify and train crisis management teams. Protocols are useless if people haven't been trained to apply them. Make sure your first responders are trained in first aid and triage. Make sure your communicators are trained in communicating in a crisis so people know whom to contact when and when to trigger crisis management protocols.

One of the learnings from the Boeing 737 Max crashes is that their crisis management protocols should have been triggered years before they were. It seems that some knew there was a potential problem and chose not to deal with it.

Pre-positioning human, financial, and operational resources. People need direction, training, and resources. Make sure there's a site leader at each of your sites with access to cash. Make sure your first responders have working first-aid kits.

React to Events

Our fight or flight instincts evolved to equip us for moments like this. If the team has the capabilities and capacity in place, turn it loose to respond to the events. This is where all the hard work of preparation pays off.

A big part of this is knowing when and how to react without under- or overreacting.

Bridge the Gaps

While first responders should react in line with their training, keep in mind that random, instinctual, uncoordinated actions by multiple groups exacerbate chaos. Stopping everything until excruciatingly detailed situation assessments have been fed into excruciatingly detailed plans that get approved by excruciatingly excessive layers of management leads to things happening excruciatingly too late.

The preferred methodology is to pause before you accelerate to get thinking and plans vaguely right quickly. Then, get going to bridge the gaps with a combination of discipline (structure, doctrine, process) and agility (creativity, improvisation, adaptability).[5]

Situational questions (Keeping in mind the physical, political, emotional context.)

- What do we know and not know about what happened and its impact (facts)?
- What are the implications of what we know and don't know (conclusions)?
- What do we predict may happen (scenarios)?

---

[5] Ibid.

- What resources and capabilities do we have at our disposal (assets)? Gaps?
- What aspects of the situation can we turn to our advantage?

Objectives and Intent

Armed with answers to those questions, think through and choose the situational objectives and intent. What are the desired outcomes of leading through the crisis? What is the desired end state? This is a critical component of direction and a big deal.

For example, when the aforementioned glass water bottle capper went bad, grinding screw top threads into glass chips, the objective and intent were (1) stop the damage and (2) protect the brand.

Priorities

The Red Cross provides relief to victims of disasters. In doing that, the prioritization of shelter, food, water, medicine, and emotional support varies by the type of disaster. If someone's home is destroyed by a fire in the winter, shelter takes precedence. On the other hand, if a reservoir gets contaminated, the critical priority is getting people clean water.

These examples illustrate the importance of thinking through the priorities for each individual situation and each stage of a developing crisis. The choices for isolating, containing, controlling, and stabilizing the immediate situation likely will be different than the priorities for the mid-term response, which is more about getting resources in the right place and then delivering the required support over time. Those in turn will be different from the priorities involved in repairing the damage from the crisis or disaster and preventing its reoccurrence.

Get the answer to the question, "Where do we focus our efforts first?" and the priority choices start to become clear. Then, get them communicated to all, perhaps starting with a set of meetings to:

- Recap current situation and needs and what has already been accomplished
- Agree on objectives, intent, priorities, and phasing of priorities

- Agree on action plans, milestones, role sort, communication points, plans, and protocols

These are the same building blocks discussed in the body of this book. However, a crisis is better managed by using an iterative approach than by using the more sequential approach. This is why we recommend early meetings to jump-start strategic, operational, and organizational processes all at the same time, getting things vaguely right quickly and then adapting to new information along the way.

Bridge the Gap Between the Desired and Current State

Support team members in implementing plans while gathering more information concurrently.

Complete situation assessment and mid-term prioritization and plans.

Conduct milestone update sessions daily or more frequently as appropriate.

- Update progress on action plans with focus on wins, learning, areas needing help.
- Update situation assessment.
- Adjust plans iteratively, reinforcing the expectation of continuous adjustment.

Overcommunicate at every step of the way to all the main constituencies. Your message and main communication points will evolve as the situation and your information about the situation evolve. This makes the need that much greater for frequent communication updates within the organization, with partner organizations and the public. Funneling as much as possible through one spokesperson will reduce misinformation. Do not underestimate the importance of this.

Along the way and through every step, your communication should be emotional, rational, and inspirational:

- **Emotional:** Connect with your audience, empathizing with how the crisis is affecting them personally.

- **Rational:** Lay out the hard facts of the current situation in detail with a calm, composed, polite, and authoritative tone and manner.

- **Inspirational:** Inspire others by thinking ahead, painting an optimistic view of the future, and calling people to practical actions they can take to be part of the solution, which will instill confidence and calm in them.

Remember the airplane that crash landed in the Hudson River? First officer Jeff Skiles was the "pilot in charge" of the airplane when it took off, ran into a flock of birds, and lost both its engines. At that point, Captain Chesley Sullenberger chose to take over. With his command "my aircraft," followed by Skiles's "your aircraft," control (and leadership) was passed to "Sully," who safely landed the plane on the Hudson River. Only one pilot can be in charge at a time. Two people trying to steer the same plane at the same time simply does not work.

The same is true for crisis and disaster management. Only one person can be the pilot in charge of any effort or component at a time. A critical part of implementation is clarifying and reclarifying who is doing what and who is making what decisions at what point—especially as changing conditions dictate changes in roles and decision-making authority within and across organizations. Make sure the handoffs are as clean as the one on Sully and Skiles's flight.

After-Action Review

At the end of the crisis, conduct an after-action review looking at:

- What actually happened? How did that compare with what we expected to happen?

- What impact did we have? How did that compare with our objectives?

- What did we do particularly effectively that we should do again?

- What can we do even better the next time in terms of risk mitigation and response?

Onboarding in a Crisis

Any executive onboarding into a new position should converge and then evolve. They should get a head-start, manage their message, and then pivot to set direction, build the team, sustain momentum, and deliver results. However, if you're a new leader making a hot landing in the middle of a crisis, you must parallel process and (1) jump right in to help, (2) learn with everyone else, and (3) let your leadership emerge over time.[6]

In normal circumstances, asking for help onboarding into a new organization is a great way to show some vulnerability and start relationships. In a crisis, everything is turned around. People are scared, confused, and overwhelmed. They are going to appreciate you more if you come in offering help than seeking it. Be a team-oriented giver, not an individual taker.

1. **Jump right in to help.**

   In a crisis, Maslow's hierarchy resets, and everyone has to build back through the stages of physiological to safety to belonging to esteem and then self-actualization needs all over again. You have to deal with the current reality before you can focus on the future.

   Even worse, as Harvard's Dutch Leonard explained in a session on Crisis Management for Leaders, in major emergencies like COVID-19, no one knows what to do. We're all operating in an environment with far more stress, far less capacity, and far less knowledge than anyone can reasonably handle. As he puts it, effective leadership is going to require "rapid innovation under stress embedded in fear."[7]

   Everyone is at the same disadvantage because no one knows how the crisis is going to play out or what the organization is going to look like on the other side. They can't help with your onboarding. But you can provide them needed extra capacity if you focus on helping them. Make it about them at the start, not about you.

2. **Learn with everyone else.**

   Like the difference between driving in Ethiopia and Kenya discussed earlier in this book, every company drives on different

---

[6] George Bradt, 2020, "Hot Landings: Starting a New Leadership Role During a Crisis," *Forbes*, April 2.

[7] Herman B. "Dutch" Leonard et al., 2020, "Crisis Management for Leaders Coping with Covid-19," Harvard Kennedy School Program on Crisis Leadership, April.

sides of the road in different ways, and you need to learn from others in the company how things work to avoid collisions.

But in a crisis, it's like jumping into a moving car with a group of people trying to get directions while accelerating on a new road in a country they know nothing about. They're not going to slow down to give you an orientation on the rules of the road. You're all learning together. Don't ask to learn from them. Learn with them.

3. **Let your leadership emerge over time.**

The core of effective crisis leadership is iterating through the following steps, all guided by your purpose (mission, vision, values):

1. Relook at the new situation and scenarios from physical, emotional, reputational, political, and financial standpoints.

2. Agree on near-term objectives and intent. Remember to focus on physical safety first, reputation second, and financial implications third.

3. Develop options for what you might do.

4. Predict risk-weighted outcomes for each option.

5. Choose which options to prioritize.

6. For each priority, get clear on an accountable leader and what will get done by when by whom with what resources.

7. Execute, monitor, and iterate.

In a crisis, all are trying to figure out what to do together. Asking powerful questions is more valuable than pretending to have answers. Let your leadership emerge through the iterations as you learn more, clarify evolving roles and expectations, and earn others' confidence.

Think in terms of four stages: (1) listening and doing what you're asked to do; (2) providing input into the discussions; (3) making recommendations; and (4) making decisions—after you've earned that right through your work in the first three stages.

Timing your transition from stage to stage is going to be more of an art than a science. Let the evolution of your relationship with your boss and team members guide you.

Summary and Implications

Leading through a crisis is about inspiring, enabling, and empowering others to get things vaguely right quickly and adapting iteratively along the way—with clear direction, leadership, and roles. Three steps:

1. **Prepare in advance.** Preparation breeds confidence. Think through your own crisis management protocols. Pre-position resources. Identify and train crisis management teams.

2. **React to events.** Leverage that preparation to respond quickly and flexibly in the moment. This requires courage on the part of management to let people do what they prepared to do without a lot of oversupervision early on. However, it is important to instill an "ask for help early" rather than a "wait until we are overwhelmed" attitude in the responders.[8]

3. **Bridge the gaps** between desired and current situation, response capabilities, and prevention, supporting team members in implementing purpose-driven, priority-focused plans while gathering more information concurrently.

---

[8] Chris Saeger, 2010, Discussion at American Red Cross, May.

Berman, William, and Bradt, George. 2021. *Influence and Impact: Discover and Excel at What Your Organization Needs from You Most.* Hoboken, NJ: John Wiley & Sons.

Bradt, George. 2011–2022. *The New Leader's Playbook*, articles on www .Forbes.com.

Bradt, George, and Bancroft, Ed. 2010. *The Total Onboarding Program: An Integrated Approach to Recruiting, Hiring, and Accelerating Talent Facilitators.* San Francisco: Pfeiffer.

Bradt, George, and Davis, Gillian. 2014. *First-Time Leader: Foundational Tools for Inspiring and Enabling Your New Team.* Hoboken, NJ: John Wiley & Sons.

Bradt, George, and Pritchett, Jeffrey. 2022. *The Mergers & Acquisition Leader's Playbook: A Practical Guide to Integrating Organizations, Executing Strategy, and Driving New Growth after M&A or Private Equity Deals.* Hoboken, NJ: John Wiley & Sons.

Bradt, George, and Vonnegut, Mary. 2009. *Onboarding: How to Get Your New Employees Up to Speed in Half the Time.* Hoboken, NJ: John Wiley & Sons.

Brown, Brené. 2010. "The Power of Vulnerability." TED Talk video, 20:19. June. http://www.ted.com/talks/brene_brown_on_vulnerability.

Buckingham, Marcus, and Clifton, Donald. 2001. *Now, Discover Your Strengths.* New York: Free Press.

Chandran, Rajiv, de la Boutetier, Hortense, and Dewar, Carolyn. 2015. "Ascending to the C-Suite." McKinsey Insights, April. http:// www.mckinsey.com/insights/leading_in_the_21st_century/ ascending_to_the_c-suite?cid=other-eml-nsl-mip-mck-oth-1505.

Charan, Ram, Drotter, Stephen, and Noel, James. 2001. *The Leadership Pipeline: How to Build the Leadership-Powered Company.* San Francisco: Jossey-Bass.

Covey, Steven. 1989. *The 7 Habits of Highly Effective People.* New York: Simon & Schuster.

Coyne, Kevin, and Coyne, Edward. 2007. "Surviving Your New CEO." *Harvard Business Review,* May.

Crabtree, Steve. 2013. "Worldwide, 13% of Employees Are Engaged at Work," Gallup, October 8. http://www.gallup.com/poll/165269/worldwide-employees-engaged-work.aspx.

Dattner, Ben. 2011. *The Blame Game: How the Hidden Rules of Credit and Blame Determine Our Success or Failure.* With Darren Dahl. New York: Free Press.

Deutsch, Clay, and West, Andy. 2010. *Perspectives on Merger Integration.* McKinsey, June.

Duck, Jeannie Daniel. 2001. *The Change Monster: The Human Forces That Fuel or Foil Corporate Transformation and Change*. New York: Three Rivers Press.

Eliot, T. S. 1943. "Little Gidding." In *Four Quartets*. New York: Harcourt Brace Jovanovich.

Gadiesh, Orit, and Gilbert, James L. 1998. "Profit Pools: A Fresh Look at Strategy." *Harvard Business Review*, May.

Gladwell, Malcolm. 2005. *Blink: The Power of Thinking Without Thinking*. Boston: Little, Brown.

Groysberg, Boris, Hill, Andrew, and Johnson, Toby. 2010. "Which of These People Is Your Future CEO? The Different Ways Military Experience Prepares Managers for Leadership." *Harvard Business Review*, November.

Guber, Peter. 2008. "The Four Truths of the Storyteller." *Harvard Business Review*, January.

Harrald, John R. 2006. "Agility and Discipline: Critical Success Factors for Disaster Response." *The Annals of the American Academy of Political and Social Science* 604 (March): 256–272.

Hastings, Reed. 2009. "Culture." SlideShare. August 1. http://www.slideshare.net/reed2001/culture-1798664.

Heffernan, Margaret. 2012. "Why Mergers Fail." CBS Money Watch, April 24. http://www.cbsnews.com/news/why-mergers-fail/.

Hillen, John, and Nevins, Mark. 2018. *What Happens Now?: Reinvent Yourself as a Leader Before Your Business Outruns You*. SelectBooks.

Hilton, Elizabeth. 2001. "Differences in Visual and Auditory Short-Term Memory." *Undergraduate Research Journal* 4. https://www.iusb.edu/ugr-journal/static/2001/hilton.php.

Lao-tzu. 2003. *Tao Te Ching*. Translated by Jonathan Star. New York: Tarcher.

Linver, Sandy. 1983. *Speak and Get Results: The Complete Guide to Speeches and Presentations That Work in Any Business Situation*. With Nick Taylor. New York: Summit.

Maslow, Abraham H. 1943. "A Theory of Human Motivation." *Psychological Review* 50 (4): 370–96.

Masters, Brooke. 2009. "Rise of a Headhunter." *Financial Times*, March 30. www.ft.com/cms/s/0/19975256-1af2-11de-8aa3-0000779fd2ac.html.

Neff, Thomas J., and Citrin, James M. 2005. *You're in Charge, Now What? The 8 Point Plan*. New York: Crown Business.

Neilson, Gary L., Martin, Karla L., and Powers, Elizabeth. 2008, "The Secrets to Successful Strategy Execution." *Harvard Business Review*, June, 60.

Schein, Edgar. 1985. *Organizational Culture and Leadership*. San Francisco: Jossey-Bass.

Senge, Peter M. 1990. *The Fifth Discipline: The Art and Practice of the Learning Organization*. New York: Doubleday/Currency.

Senge, Peter M. 1994. *The Fifth Discipline Fieldbook: Strategies and Tools for Building a Learning Organization*. Boston: Nicholas Brealey.

Watkins, Michael. 2003. *The First 90 Days: Critical Success Strategies for New Leaders at All Levels*. Boston: Harvard Business School Press.

George Bradt has led the revolution in how people start new jobs. He progressed through sales, marketing, and general management around the world at companies including Procter & Gamble, Coca-Cola, and J.D. Power's Power Information Network spin-off as chief executive.

Now he is chair of PrimeGenesis, the executive onboarding group he founded in 2002 to accelerate complex transitions for leaders and teams. Since then, George and his partners have reduced new leader failure rates from 40 percent to less than 10 percent through a single-minded focus on helping them and teams deliver better results faster over their first 100 days.

A graduate of Harvard and Wharton (MBA), George is coauthor of 11 books on onboarding and leadership, over 750 columns on Forbes, and 19 plays and musicals (book, lyrics, and music). His e-mail address is gbradt@PrimeGenesis.com.

Other leadership and onboarding books by George:

- *The Merger & Acquisition Leader's Playbook: A Practical Guide to Integrating Organizations, Executing Strategy, and Driving New Growth after M&A or Private Equity Deals* (Wiley, 2022)

- *Influence and Impact: Discover and Excel at What Your Organization Needs from You the Most* (Wiley, 2021)

- *First-Time Leader* (Wiley, 2014)

- *Onboarding: How to Get Your New Employees Up to Speed in Half the Time* (Wiley, 2009)

- *The Total Onboarding Program: An Integrated Approach* (Wiley/Pfeiffer, 2010)

- *Point of Inflection* (GHP Press, 2022)

- *CEO Boot Camp* (GHP Press, 2019)

- *The New Job 100-Day Plan* (GHP Press, 2012)

- *The New Leader's Playbook* (GHP Press, one volume each year 2011–2021)
- *Executive Onboarding* (GHP Press, four volumes, 2020)

Jayme A. Check is founding partner of PrimeGenesis and a leading expert on senior executive transitions. He offers a global perspective on leadership gained from executive and advisory roles with Fortune 500, start-up, private equity, and venture capital firms. He is recognized for deep expertise in navigating high-growth and rapidly changing environments while leading strategic, operational, and cultural transformations. Jayme started his career on Wall Street at JP Morgan and subsequently held senior leadership positions in sales, business development, and general management at several high-growth companies.

Since 2004, Jayme has been CEO of Quantum Global Partners, a firm that provides companies worldwide with strategic direction, planning, execution, and senior interim management as well as results-based coaching and leadership development.

Jayme earned his BS from Syracuse University and his MBA from UCLA's Anderson School. His articles and opinions have appeared in *Bloomberg Businessweek*, Fox Business, and *Talent Management* magazine, among others. He is a sought-after speaker and moderator. Jayme can be reached at jcheck@PrimeGenesis.com.

John Lawler is PrimeGenesis's CEO. Previously, he was CEO of three private equity–backed companies, leading business and cultural transformations in a variety of industries. Before that, at LexisNexis, he served as group president and built a new division of high-growth legal technology businesses via acquisition, investment, and integration; as CEO of Martindale-Hubbell, he led a successful digital transformation. Earlier in his career, John was an investment banker at Bear Stearns and led transitions and growth initiatives at Dun & Bradstreet.

John is a proven leadership and business consultant, transformational CEO, board member, and coach, with a track record of tapping his experiences to help leaders accelerate growth and generate superior returns organically and via mergers and acquisitions. He has extensive experience in the Americas, Europe, and Asia. He earned his BA from Williams College and his MBA from the University of Virginia. His e-mail address is jlawler@PrimeGenesis.com.